Twin Flames and The Event

A Message for the 144,000 Lightworkers

By Jen McCarty

For permission requests, contact the author Jen McCarty - info@jenmccarty.co.uk

Book Front Page Cover Artist: Cheryl Yambrach Rose

First Print Edition 14/02/2021

ISBN–978-1-8383941-0-3

Disclaimer Notice:

Although the author has made every effort to ensure that the information in this book was correct at time of press, the author does not assume and hereby disclaims any liability to any party for any loss, damage, or disruption caused by errors or omissions, whether such errors or omissions result from negligence, accident, or any other cause.

This book is not intended as a substitute for the medical advice of physicians. The reader should regularly consult a physician in matters relating to his/her health and particularly with respect to any symptoms that may require diagnosis or medical attention.

Message from Jen: All of the information that I share has been received directly through my own access to the Akashic Records. Nothing that I share is regurgitated information; it is all based on downloads that I have personally received. It is so important that as you are reading these words, you exercise your own discernment and only take on as truth that which resonates for you as truth. If something does not feel true to you, then that is correct; so please do honour that.

I have been guided to speak about subject matters such as Kundalini Energy, Twin Flames, Hieros Gamos, the Zero-Point Field and Fifth Dimensional Consciousness many times in many different ways throughout this book. The reason for the constant repetition of these subject matters is to act as an antidote to the heavy third dimensional programming that has sought to indoctrinate everyone into the false belief that they are simply limited to the third dimension. This book is a reprogramming agenda of the highest order, and the way that it is delivered to you is encoded with specific intentions.

PUBLISHED BY;

I dedicate this book to my beloved.

Table of Contents

ACKNOWLEDGEMENTS

I would like to now give my personal thanks to all the people that have helped me bring this book to the world. The first person I would like to thank is my personal assistant Zoe, for all of her help in formatting the book and structuring the chapters and doing all the back pages and front pages and generally being the best friend anyone could ever wish for.

I would also like to thank Pippa Harrison for her incredible role in the final edit of the book. Thank you to Stephen Lomax for supporting me with the initial edit as we started the project and thank you so much to Laura Savill for doing the final proofread at the end.

I would also like to thank Kelly Jones for her incredible designer capabilities and skills in creating such a beautiful front cover and back cover and I would like to thank Kyra Kelm for her support in bringing the Workbook to you all.

I would also like to say thank you to Cheryl Yambrach Rose for providing the exquisite painting on the front cover and I would sincerely like to thank my beautiful dear soul sister, Laura Eisenhower, for sharing with us the powerful afterword for the book. I would also like to thank Gloria Coppola for helping me with the promotion of my book.

I would like to acknowledge my son Fin for supporting me throughout this whole project, and for being a shining example of a truly embodied divine masculine.

I would also like to acknowledge my mother and the fine job she did at bringing up such a God-loving daughter.

I would like to thank her for all of the unconditional love that she has embodied, teaching me the truth about God through motherly love.

There are so many people that have helped me - all of my street team (those that read the first four chapters of the book in order to give me a review for Amazon) and all of my translators.

There are no words that can adequately express how grateful I am to every person that has come forward to support me in bringing this powerful book to the world, especially my son Finn. The universe has blessed me with the most extraordinary example of the divine masculine, he is my greatest teacher and one of my soul's best friends.

I'm really sorry if I've missed anyone. You're in my heart and I truly am so grateful to you.

A guru is a light in the darkness. This book would not have been born without my gurus, especially BaBaJi. I refer to a guru as a soulmate who is always there for you in the deepest darkness. I would like to thank all my spiritual teachers especially Louise Hay, Candice O'Denver and Shakti Gawain. In the spirit of these deep acknowledgments, I must truly also thank the Christ and the Magdalene flame that dwells eternally within me.

Regardless of where you are on your spiritual path, whether you be a beginner or a seasoned explorer into the deepest mysteries of existence, the words in this book will awaken memories in you that have long been sleeping - memories of your true and abiding divinity.

The words are organised in such a way that it can be likened to light language and light codes.

These words transcend the boundaries of time and space and align immediately with your heart's consciousness.

The key to Christ consciousness is through the heart.

BOOK TESTIMONIES FOR TWIN FLAMES

AND THE EVENT

Jen,

I just finished reading the first four chapters of your book. Thank you so much for this opportunity for my soul to bask in your beautiful love and wisdom. It truly is a gift to me and will be as well to whoever reads your words.

I cried so many tears because I knew without a shadow of a doubt that every single word is true. My heart and soul are at peace and I feel as if I am wrapped in a blanket of love. Through your words, I feel so dearly loved and protected by our Creator.

I am so happy to be on this journey with you and to be a Twin Flame and Starseed who is ready to put on her crown so others know their own Divinity as well. A beautiful read thus far and a true blessing to all of humanity. Thank you from the bottom of my heart.

Blessings,
Sheila Jenkins
Author of *The Day Before: Eternal Bonds into the Afterlife*
Infinite Love: 50 Twin Soul Love Quotes

Jen,

My life has been extremely difficult with so much trauma. Your book is helping me out of deep despair that I am currently facing with so much coming up that I never knew in repressed memories/flashbacks. Below is my review. Thank you for all that you do beautiful Jen!

After a lifelong struggle of working to overcome the effects of extreme abuse in my childhood, I have arrived at perhaps the most challenging period of my life, facing PTSD, flashback after flashback, and just so much pain. I write this now because I want to say that this book, TWIN FLAMES AND THE EVENT, has come to me in the midst of this processing.

I didn't know if I could even concentrate on the book, each line, or each word. But guidance said, "Read, even just one sentence for now." So I did! As I read, starting from the very first word of the prologue, I felt hope coming back! I felt God within me warm my heart and fill my soul! I felt the remembrance and knowing of the truth in each line; that even in the chaos of all of this that I am experiencing, I am "the lighthouse" that I had once promised that I would be.

I had felt so mired in my life circumstances (have also experienced chronic illness for 20+ years), that I had felt my faith slipping away. Yet, as I read Jen McCarty's words, "It is absolutely and purely about faith," I felt the living, loving, Divine frequencies encoded in these words!

My heart embraced them and enveloped them very peacefully and lovingly! It's really quite challenging to describe the experience of reading this incredible book! Jen was not kidding when she said, "In this book, every word is specifically directed to support you to very swiftly align with the Spiritual master-avatar being that you truly are - the galactic, angelic, timeless, off-spring of eternal love."

I am writing about just a small portion of these beautiful, sacred, holy gifts that are encoded energetically in each and every word! There is just so much to say about this book that I could go on for quite some time. Suffice it to say that over the past 20+ years of my spiritual journey, I have purchased countless good books, but I honestly feel that this one is superior to all of those.

Jen McCarty has channelled a book like no other! Once I started my "one sentence" in which I had been guided, I did not want to stop. Not only is this book filled with ancient wisdom, but it is also a dynamic Divine experience.

I know that I will read and re-read this many times, as I have already started my second reading. Immense gratitude, Jen McCarty! This book will change countless lives! I know it's changing mine!

Transformative, Beautiful, Relatable, Divine! What a gift!

Jill Sutter

We are truly free when we are lucid in God's dream

PROLOGUE

Before me, I was shown a scene where I stood as a soul before Mother-Father God. In that scene, I could see that I had the choice of multiple different life paths ahead of me. They were displayed as mountain paths and peaks ranging in size and beauty.

I was shown that at that moment, where that choice was given, my soul very courageously stepped forward and said, "I choose to take the path with the highest peaks and the most exquisite vistas."

At this point, Mother-Father God came close and said... "My child, you truly are one of my most courageous beloved children, but I must forewarn you that this path that you choose is a most challenging one. As on this path, many times you will feel alone and abandoned by me. As all around you, you will see others who have taken the less high paths and things will seem easy for them.

"But my child, the one that you have chosen, is the one that delivers you back to your full ascended Union with your beloved Twin Flame. This will ensure the anchoring of the new paradigm of sacred relationship, deeply into the core of Mother Earth.

"Taking this path means that whenever you seek outside yourself for love, through relationships, substances, food - or any addictions, you will never find it. This is how I have created it to be. It is only by turning back to me, turning back to yourself, that you will ever find the solace, comfort and love that you seek.

"There will not be many people on Earth at this time who have chosen this path. You will be blazing a trail. You are one of the way-showers. This path will be very, very hard for your ego and you will feel angry at me when you can't manifest the love that you are seeking from outside of yourself.... Beloved child of my heart, are you sure you want to choose this path?"

And my soul in all her courage and bravery said, "Yes God, I choose that path, as taking that path will be my greatest service to humanity. That is my heart's intention: to serve humanity. The needs of my ego are insignificant to me," and God replied, "You say that now my child, but it won't feel like that. You can still opt for the easier path, whereby you will meet a soulmate early on in life and you will create an easy and comfortable life together.

"You will have some challenges, but at the end of your lifetime you will not have attained the spiritual insights and wisdom that the higher path will offer you, as you will not have had to face your shadow self, your ego or the void within you. Indeed, this easier path will prevent you from coming as deeply home to me, but it will be easy and comfortable."

"But God, how will I be able to come back to you? How will I know how to turn to you? Will you show me and guide me in the ways that I can truly turn back to you, as my saviour, my guide, my home, my sanctuary?"

"Yes, my child, I will be able to show you how to do that, as your connection with me will be so lucid and pristine, it will be easy for me to reveal that to you."

"So, tell me now God, how do I do that, how do I turn to you?"

"My sweet, sweet child, your willingness to turn to me is 99% of it. Your willingness is symbolic of your failing at finding love outside of yourself, and when you have failed at that, you will turn back to me.

"There will be homesickness on your path, where you will cease to be gratified by external sources of love, and that will be deeply painful for you and your inner child - but remembering who I am, and your connection to me, is your salvation.

"You will remember that I have my arms eternally outstretched before you and am ever beckoning you back home to my heart, and your memory of that will bring you back to me.

"My precious child, your task on this Earth is to remember that you are seen and held, adored, comforted, protected and filled by me. As you remember that deeply, you will be carried up this seemingly treacherous path with great ease, and you will automatically attract your beloved from the space of alignment and divine perfection.

"The love that is your destiny is a direct reflection of the love I have for you. I love you beyond words, beyond sentiments, beyond ideas. When you know and rest in this love and truly deeply know it from the depths of your being, then and only then can it be reflected outside of yourself.

"You, my sweet child, are on track now to reach this most stunning vista that we have co-created together and it comes from all of this hard work and discipline that you have diligently committed to.

"Well done, my sweet, sweet child; I rejoice in your remembrance of my deep love for you, as you remember how your cup is filled and is overflowing, and that the deep void that is the hallmark of the ego self- is filled, not from a substance outside of itself, but from

"I Am that I Am - God Source Within."

INTRODUCTION

I met an Astrologer recently. He looked at my chart and was blown away by what he saw. He said that on the 21st of December 2020, Jupiter transits Saturn at nought degrees Aquarius, and this day marks the true birth of the Age of Aquarius. He said to me that my Aquarius in my natal chart is between nought and one degree Aquarius. So, this means that this date will be extremely significant for me and my evolutionary journey.

It was quite a life-changing experience having this destined meeting with this Astrologer and it set me off on a course which led me to find out a great deal about what was going on planetarily in this time of the great shift.

This week has been very auspicious for me, as the 14-year platform that I had built up on Facebook was taken down, as was my Instagram with well over 150,000 dedicated followers. I had tirelessly built up this community from scratch, consistently sharing posts and messages that would automatically activate DNA and bring about lasting transformation in one's consciousness.

Losing this platform was initially very challenging for me, as it made me question how I would rebuild my community again. But something extremely wonderful has come out of this, and that is, that it has given me space to finally create the book that you hold in your hands now. A lasting legacy that will remain forever.

And so, here you have it in your hands, the book that has been brewing inside of me for many, many years. When they took away my social media platforms, it was obvious to me that it was time for me to create my book explaining the significance of the role of twin flames in this current planetary Ascension.

As many of you in my community are already aware, I experienced the Ascension of my consciousness in October 2013, four days before my 40th birthday. On that fateful date, I received a powerful vision of my divine consort's true identity. When his identity was revealed to me on the inner planes of consciousness, it fully and completely activated the Ascension of my consciousness and triggered an almighty Kundalini awakening.

I then went on to experience the Hieros Gamos, the inner alchemical union; the Kundalini merge of myself with my divine creator and all that is. When this phenomenon happened for me, I knew that what I was experiencing was hugely impacting the world and indeed the entire universe energetically.

I knew without a shadow of a doubt that I had arrived at the place that all souls seek in their evolutionary sojourns on planet Earth. I had arrived at the place of divine, sacred, and eternal union with God source/all that is, and this triggered the identity of my true Twin Flame to be revealed to me on the inner planes of consciousness.

When I saw his face, my soul deeply recognised him and this activated codons in my DNA to fire up, that had previously been dormant. These codons were connected to the highest realms of consciousness that are possible to reach as a human being. From that experience, I started receiving download after download about Twin Flames and their role with regards to the upcoming planetary Ascension.

So, here you have it, my book, the one I have been waiting to write, and the book that many of you have been waiting to read.

In this book, I will share with all of you what my spirit team showed me about:

- The origins of Twin Flames
- How to merge with your Twin Flame
- The role of Twin Flames in this upcoming Ascension
- What Ascension is
- What is happening to this planet currently in this Ascension window
- The Upcoming solar flash "Event"

I will speak in-depth about how the solar flash event is directly related to humanity's consciousness, specifically the number of successful Twin Flame unions that have anchored on the earthly plane.

CHAPTER ONE - WHAT IS A TWIN FLAME?

I was shown that at the beginning of creation, all that existed was a white ovoid sphere of light. This sphere of light existed in its singularity for trillions and trillions of what we would term earthly years and at some point, it was decided within this singular void of light, that it would split in order to experience itself.

When this primary and original split occurred, it could never be possible that Mother-Father God would create masculine and feminine polarities separately. For the masculine and feminine energy is one and can never be energetically separated. Indeed, it can be likened to two sides of the same coin. It is simply impossible to only have one side of a coin, and it is the same with masculine and feminine energy; they cannot be created individually from source energy or co-exist independently.

I was shown that in the moment of that first original split from source energy, as the souls separated they were androgynous in nature. These androgynous souls were comprised of a polarity of masculine and feminine energy, each containing identical soul signatures.

When this original split occurred, it was decreed that we, as an androgynous pair, would stay in our unified state for eons. And whilst we co-existed in this androgynous state, we were allowed to explore many different aspects of our universe and planetary systems.

At some point within this androgynous singularity, it was decreed that the original masculine and feminine pair (who had remained in an entirely androgynous state up until this point) would split, in order to create two individualised aspects: One masculine and one feminine polarised energetic unit.

This was allowed to take place in order to create an experience of separation for the two polarities, that they may move about the universe, learning, growing and expanding, based upon their own individual experiences.

This would ensure that when they come back together again after aeons of separation, the most extraordinary vibrations of bliss would be activated, throughout the entire universe, triggered through the rapturous joy of their inevitable reunion.

It was known by the highest forces of light that once this original pair who held and contained the same identical soul signature or tonal resonance were reunited back together again, they would contribute their vast experiences and ultimate expansion towards their unified androgynous soul unit, and this would ultimately contribute - absolutely and profusely- to the expansion of the universe as a whole.

I will go into more detail about soul groups and the monadic structure of soul groups. For now, it is important that I share with you the above introduction as to what is a Twin Flame, from the perspective of being shown by my higher self.

Please know that in this book I will return to this original description a few times, as a way to keep reinforcing this truthful remembrance programming, back into the forefront of your heart consciousness.

All of the information that I share has been received directly through my access to the Akashic Records. Nothing that I share is regurgitated information. It is all based on downloads that I have personally received.

I am not claiming any of this to be the absolute truth. This is simply one child of God's experience of life on Earth. Please always use your own discernment to decide whether this message resonates with you and feels true to you.

I have brought through a very, very powerful workbook that goes alongside this book. It would serve you well to do all of the meditations and exercises that I share in the workbook, as they have been specifically designed to assist you to become one with your higher self, so that you may attract your Twin Flame quickly and efficiently.

Please know that for those of you who are drawn to this work - you are invariably a part of the 144,000 Starseed, Twin Soul collective. Therefore, it is a spiritual fact that you are in eternal and perpetual connection with your divine eternal consort: your Twin Flame on the inner and higher dimensional planes of consciousness.

Coming Home to Christ Consciousness

When I was 21, I went to India for the first time and I was guided to meet a very significant soulmate of mine on my spiritual journey. I was told by my spirit team that I would be meeting someone with the spiritual name Christopher and indeed the day came when I did meet this person.

This was an extremely highly ordained meeting, which activated an extraordinary recognition and alchemy, and triggered my first Kundalini awakening.

This activated the blasting open of my third eye on top of that Himalayan mountain in 1995. I remembered the truth of God consciousness. I remembered that I am an eternal child of God and I remembered that you are an eternal child of God.

I remembered that every single blade of grass, every single grain of sand is sacred. Every single aspect of creation was weaved perfectly into the tapestry of All That Is. And if that one grain of sand wasn't there, there would be a lack in the fabric of creation.

In that experience I was shown through my soul brother, whom I was guided to meet as a catalyst for this awakening experience; who I am, and indeed who we all are.

When I looked into his eyes for the first time, I truly, absolutely saw Christopher, the Christ-Self within him. And because I could see it so distinctly staring back at me from him, I knew implicitly that this was a reflection of myself. And in that moment, I woke to the truth that I am the Christ. He is the Christ. And therefore, that automatically means that every single one of us is Christ. Every single being alive is equally loved, equally cherished by our creator self.

Mother-Father God has no favourites, no specials, regardless of how advanced you are on your spiritual path, that means nothing to Mother-Father God, as Mother-Father God is a great God and does not have favourites. We are all equally loved, we are all equally precious children of

God and we all hold the Christ-Self within us. It's just a case of each of us recognising that in each other.

In the moment, on top of that mountain, where my third eye blasted open, I often say to people nowadays that I experienced an overdose of God. Most souls sign up to get a spoonful of God remembrance, some sign up for a cup, but I definitely signed up for the whole entire bottle!

And that is why I come here speaking these words to all of you. It was 25 years ago that I had that experience and it has taken me a very, very long time for me to come out and share my message of what I have been shown to the world. Sharing the truth that I consider to be such an auspicious blessing, to have had that experience with God.

I will be speaking about this subject matter much more in my upcoming autobiography about my spiritual awakenings. So, thank you all so much for jumping on board this exciting and inspirational train of spreading these words far and wide to Africa, to India, to Russia, to China.

It is time for us to remember that we are children of God and Mother-Father God created this playground for us to dance and to play. And ultimately, truly to dance and play with our best friend, our eternal best friend throughout all of creation. This is what the design of creation specifically has been all about.

The third dimensional matrix has sought to eradicate, tamper with and create a filter to the remembrance of the truth, that we are all here to have this high and ecstatic dance with our most precious and beloved soul partner in the universe.

So, may these sacred words remind you that you are not alone, that you are in eternal fifth dimensional union with your divine counterpart. And that your union is active and alive on the fifth dimensional realm of consciousness and above and is indeed sealed in the zero-point field.

Your divine counterpart exists within your very heart and within your own Kundalini energy. And you can contact your divine counterpart if you are not in physical union, through listening very deeply to your heart when you send forth telepathic messages to your beloved.

And then, remembering that the secret is to not only listen to the voice of your heart but to actually believe the message that the heart reveals.

You must have ears that are sensitive to listen to what your heart is saying. And that is why the word heart contains the word ear, because we must listen to our heart as that is where you will hear your beloved speaking messages of eternal love, friendship, protection, laughter, light, marriage and eternal bliss.

It turns out that Christopher was my catalyst twin, and I will speak in depth about catalyst twins later on in this book. Unfortunately he has left his body now and returned back to the Godhead. As soon as he arrived back home with God he contacted me telepathically, and gave me an extremely powerful message about how monadic soul structures are formed, which I will write about in the upcoming chapter.

Monadic Soul Structures

I would like to share with you all now what I have been shown about monadic soul structures.

I was shown by my spirit team (via my catalyst twin who passed over) that each monadic soul group is comprised of 144 Souls - 72 masculine and 72 feminine polarity Twin Soul resonant pairs, also known as identical tonal partners.

My team went on to show me that the 144 monadic structure splits into six soul pods, comprised of 12 masculine and 12 feminine polarities. You can imagine it as the divine masculines making an outer ring of 12 harmonic frequencies with their identical counterparts standing directly opposite them, making the inner circle of 12 resonant, divine feminines; each of them holding the identical, opposite polarity to their divine counterpart.

This then breaks down to a set of 24 souls, which is your innermost Soul group. This comprises of 12 masculine and 12 feminine Twin Soul resonant pairs, who stand with you as your closest vibratory soul brothers and sisters in creation.

Spirit showed me that as the soul descends from the Godhead, God holds a perfect 144 resonant fractal patterning, and as we are all fractals of God we are all carrying that identical 144 patterning within our Merkabic field.

This breaks down to our 144 soul group, our inner circle of 24 and ultimately the vibratory frequency and resonance between you and your beloved Twin Flame. This is the one that stands opposite you in the circle of 12 pairs.

I would like to add here that it is very important that you visualise the circle of 12 feminine polarity Twins, standing opposite their true tonal counterpart masculine Twin souls.

The soul that stands next to your divine masculine (if you are a divine feminine) is what you would term your

Catalyst Twin, also known as your near Twin or False Twin. I will speak about this in greater depth, later in this book.

The Catalyst Twin soul contract is a very powerful soul contract. This is a soul that you will have been in a relationship with in many lifetimes; possibly, even more lifetimes than you have been with your Twin Flame.

This is why so many on the spiritual path get lost in the belief that their Catalyst Twin is their true Twin. I had that experience for many, many years. It wasn't until my Catalyst Twin left his body and fully ascended back to spirit that I was truly able to let him go.

As soon as he returned back to the Godhead he came through with a very powerful channeled message, and he told me about the mechanics of how monadic soul structures work.

Do All Souls Have a Twin?

It has been shown to me that all souls have a Twin, but all souls do not remember that they have a Twin, nor are they soul contracted to unite with their Twin in this lifetime.

All souls are created as Twins because the masculine and feminine energy cannot be separated from itself. The masculine and feminine energy are literally two sides of the same coin and it is simply not possible to have only one side of a coin.

At some point within the unit's evolutionary trajectory, it was decreed that the individuated Twins would split from each other in order to have their own unique experiences, be that on other planets, other star systems, and including Earth.

A really great analogy to explain Twin Flames is a computer hard drive. My spirit team showed me that both Twins share the same hard drive (i.e. their subconscious mind). So, when they are in their individualised forms, all of their unique experiences are gathered and stored in their shared hard drive in order to be added to their joint evolutionary experience.

For example, if one of the Twins fully transcends the need for other people's approval, all of those codes will be stored in their joint hard drive. Then in the moment of their Union, the other Twin will have full access to these codes and will experience an extremely accelerated alignment with this way of being that has already been mastered by their Twin Flame/divine counterpart.

On a soul level, in each subsequent lifetime, we each decide before our incarnation whether we will unite with our Twin in the physical form.

If I ever get asked the question *does everyone have a Twin?* I will often say that if you have found me and my work and the potency of this sacred message, then there is a strong chance, in my humble opinion, that you are a Twin and are soul contracted to unite with your twin flame in this lifetime.

Therefore, this book and these teachings have more than likely been soul contracted with your higher self to fully awaken you to the truth of who you are, through the activating of memories that are stored in your heart consciousness and within your DNA geometric patterning.

Twin Flame Union

In the next chapter in this book, I would like to share what I have been shown about the difference between soulmate/Twin Flame and karmic relationships. I will also speak in depth about Catalyst Twin connections.

Hopefully, the message that I am about to share will bring forth a great deal of clarification for many of you. I will detail the different types of relationships that exist, particularly in the third-dimensional realm of consciousness. The reason why I am guided to add this chapter into this book is that the types of relationship that we choose can either awaken us or send us back to sleep spiritually.

Much of this book is devoted to sharing my most profound insights into what a Twin Flame relationship is. Suffice to say; your Twin Flame is your very, very best friend in the entire Multiverse.

When you have found your Twin Flame, you would never dream for one single second that there could be anyone better in this entire universe for you to spend every second and every single breath of your whole entire existence with.

When you are in union with your Twin Flame, your Twin soul, your best friend, you will also feel the vibration of heaven. This will come forward as a blissful, rapturous, continuous feeling. A knowing that you are experiencing heaven on Earth.

When you are in a Twin Flame union, your search is over. You wake up every single morning giving thanks - getting on your knees and giving thanks to the great force of love that has brought you your eternal best friend.

The synchronicities that have led you together will be of such a high calibre that they will put all Hollywood movies to shame. The depth and intensity of how you have been woven into each other's lives, from the very moment of your existence, will be absolutely jaw-dropping for every person who is blessed to witness your divine love story.

You will find in this person your greatest teacher, your eternal best friend, the sexiest lover your imagination could ever conceive, and the person whose hand you will want to hold forever and ever.

Staring in front of you are the eyes that you have been searching eternity for. In every cell of your being, you will know deeply that your search is over, and this feeling of homecoming will be continuous and perpetual.

You will never want to be out of this person's presence. Even one or two hours away from each other will be an issue. The logic is that you have waited since the time of Atlantis to finally come back together in eternal union. So why waste one more single moment apart?

Every soul holds within their heart's blueprint, the map to unite them with their Twin Flame. But not every soul has chosen this path, as it is a very challenging and arduous path. You will have to do the work on yourself, on your inner being to polish yourself, to become the most magnetic version of yourself, that will instantly attract your Twin soul back into your reality. Some souls do not sign up for the Twin Flame template; they sign up for a Soulmate template.

I spoke earlier about how each soul group is comprised of 144 Souls; 72 masculine and 72 feminine souls, standing in two concurrent circles opposite each other. Each Twin Flame tonal pair is standing opposite its divine counterpart, within the monadic soul group's structure.

We only have one Twin Flame, and that is the soul who stands opposite us in this configuration.

Catalyst Twins

The soul who is standing next to your divine counterpart within your own individual soul group is called your Catalyst Twin, sometimes known as your False Twin. Also known as your near Twin. In the majority of our lifetimes on the earthly plane, we have been married to our near Twin, as the energies of planet Earth have been far too dense to be able to hold the frequency of true Twins in harmonious union.

When we meet our Catalyst Twin, we experience an extraordinary amount of synchronicities with them. Many of us also experience the feeling of being at home, spiritually in their presence. There will also be many numerological alignments, showing us that our souls have been working together in unison for a very long time.

What I have learned about the Catalyst Twin's role is that they are sent to us before we meet our genuine Twin soul counterpart in order to assist us in preparing the garden of our heart for this eternal sacred union. Before the meeting with the Catalyst Twin, (for the most part) the garden of the heart is in quite a messy state, with many overgrown weeds and lots of rubbish to be cleared.

The Catalyst Twin (what with all the synchronicities and seeming signs from the universe that you have found the one) provides an incredible and necessary momentum for us to truly get our hands dirty; to start pulling out the weeds of old thought forms that are no longer serving us (which for the most part) many of us have inherited from our familial ancestral lineages.

The Catalyst Twin helps us very deeply prepare the garden of our heart for the seeds that the true Twin Flame is destined to bring us. Many people believe that the Catalyst Twin is the true Twin, but one of the hallmarks of this relationship is a feeling that it will never be resolved, you will never be together. No matter what you do, it just won't work.

Another hallmark of the Catalyst Twin connection is that it will trigger many of your deepest primal fears of abandonment for the divine feminine and many of the deepest primal fears of guilt and shame for the divine masculine.

The issue is that when we meet our Catalyst Twins, we are often incredibly seduced into the idea that they are our genuine Twin. But the universe knows that we can only go so far, vibrationally and spiritually, with our Catalyst Twin.

Because we are now in the turning of the great cycle and the lifetime that precipitates that, Mother-Father God requires as many genuine Twin Flames as possible to be in physical union, in order to lift the planet out of the third dimension into the fifth dimension.

When we are in a relationship with our Catalyst Twin, we can't reach the highest peaks of rapture and bliss that we can achieve with our true Twin Flame. This is why many of us have decreed to not be in these relationships in this lifetime.

The Catalyst Twin relationship is connected to soulmate relationships. A soulmate relationship is a relationship with one of the members of your 144 soul group. You will have travelled many lifetimes with this person in the form of Mother / Father / Daughter / Sister / Grandmother / Twin / Brother / Lover. It is important to remember that we have all experienced many, many lifetimes and our soulmates are the characters that we choose to incarnate with on repetitive reincarnation cycles.

A Soulmate Relationship

A soulmate relationship could be likened to finding and wearing a comfortable pair of slippers or wearing your most comfortable dressing gown. This relationship will not push you to face your deepest, darkest shadow aspects and it will not push you to become one with your higher self.

Soulmate relationships keep you at a particular vibrational level whereby you experience a certain level of comfort within your soul, but you do not experience the wild, expansive bliss that comes from uniting with the eternal best friend that your soul has sought from the moment you split from each other.

Karmic Relationships

I would like to take a moment to speak about what I have been shown about karmic relationships.

We attract karmic relationships when we have not entered into the zero-point field of consciousness and are still running-lack based programs such as:

'I will never find my true love.'

'This realm could not possibly be heaven on Earth.'

'I better just accept whatever comes my way.'

'I'll just settle for anyone who can put up with me.'

All of these thought forms are indicative of a karmic relationship.

We attract a karmic relationship based upon the vibration of survival and lack; when we have entirely forgotten the memo that Mother-Father God created this playground (which is fully templated with heavenly codes and frequencies) so that her divine children may be in perpetual bliss and eternal union with their best friend in the universe.

Most people who settle for karmic relationships have genuinely given up on the idea or even the possibility that true love is a reality.

Karmic relationships are the hallmarks of someone settling for much, much less than what their heart truly seeks and desires, and indeed what their soul consciousness has lined up for them in their spiritual destiny.

If you are reading these words and feel a little bit hot and sweaty and somewhat uncomfortable, then the chances are you are in a karmic relationship. If that is the case, now would be an excellent time for you to make a conscious choice about whether this relationship is serving your soul's most profound expansion.

Most karmic relationships manifest due to unconscious programming; however the moment an unconscious program becomes conscious, it no longer becomes a program, it now becomes a choice.

This is an invitation for you to take a moment to tune into your heart consciousness, for your heart is the GPS that will guide you to the love of your life. Your heart knows who this person is, your heart knows how to contact this person, and your heart knows that this person will be available to you, as soon as you reach out to them.

It is time now for everyone reading these words to turn down the constant voice of the mind-led egoic narrative, which is obsessed with the idea of obligation and false notions of what should and should not occur.

Too many of us ignore our heart's voice to the detriment of everyone we love. When we ignore our heart in essence, we move out of the flow of existence and move into lower dimensional timelines/experiences.

When we make choices that are not heart-based or soul-based this has a knock-on effect on everyone in our lives. Our false notion of obligation keeps everyone entrapped on lower timelines.

Therefore, this is an invitation for you right now to make a conscious choice.

Do you wish to stay in this comfortable yet extremely unexciting relationship? One whereby you can guarantee that person will be there for you when you get home from work, but will not inspire passion, poetry and a 24-hour day love making?!

The choice is yours.

Your heart is encoded to unite with your highest soul partner in existence, but this is a choice that only you can make. If you choose to ignore the voice of your heart and keep listening to the voice of your head, you are holding up the experience of bliss and rapture for the entire universe.

Karmic relationships are part of the third-dimensional paradigm and we will not be taking third-dimensional karmic relationships into the new Earth. We will only be taking with us childlike relationships built upon innocence, authenticity and the most extraordinary levels of bliss.

As ever there is so much to speak about on this subject, but this is enough for now. I do hope that this has brought you some further clarity on this very, very complex and in-depth subject.

My Personal Ascension Experience

I will share more in my upcoming books about my Kundalini awakening. Still, it does bear mentioning here that I have been very blessed to experience two life-changing Kundalini awakenings in my lifetime.

My first Kundalini awakening was when I was aged 21 on top of the Himalayan mountains in northern India while chanting the mantra ***Om Namah Shivaya.***

I experienced the second Ascension of my consciousness four days before my 40th birthday in 2013, when I had the experience of truly, genuinely arriving home in the zero-point field of consciousness.

As this homecoming occurred, I absolutely, deeply and implicitly understood and started experiencing the reality of timelines; what a timeline is and how a timeline is created. I understood irrefutably that the third-dimensional construct of time (as we had been taught) was a complete and utter fallacy. It was indeed a construct of the third dimension, created to imprison God's most Holy and divine creation in a false idea of limitation.

My second Ascension experience was triggered by awakening to the recognition of my Twin Flame on the inner planes, four days before my 40th birthday. On that fateful day, my Twin Flame appeared to me on the inner planes of consciousness and his true identity was revealed to me; this activated an almighty Kundalini awakening, the second one in my lifetime, which then triggered the Activation within me of the inner alchemical marriage, which is known as the Hieros Gamos.

The Hieros Gamos refers to the sacred union of the Kundalini serpents that were previously dormant at the base of the spine; awakening and rising in eternal recognition of each other and rushing together in perpetual and sacred union. Once this occurs, the unified energies at the base of the spine then rise up through all of the energy centres (chakras), cleaning out and purging all the programs that do not align with true divine love.

As I saw who this person was with my inner eyes, it activated codes of remembrance in my DNA that had been waiting for this moment to be released. In my remembrance and recognition of him, all of the codes of my own abiding Christ-ness and divinity were fully and wholly restored by recognising my beloved twin soul on the inner planes of consciousness and remembering the role that we have contracted to play out within the collective.

This experience was incredibly life-changing for me. I had the experience of my consciousness elevating to an extraordinarily high level whereby sacred mysteries were revealed to me, pertaining to the true role and the true nature of the masculine and feminine energies.

CHAPTER TWO - SPIRITUAL DYNAMICS BETWEEN THE MASCULINE AND FEMININE

I would like to now speak about what I've been shown about the true spiritual dynamics between the masculine and the feminine. I was shown that oftentimes energetically, it is the divine feminine that signs up to be the one who awakens first in a Twin Flame unit. At this point, it is worth noting that someone in a male body could be holding the feminine polarity within the Twin Flame relationship and vice versa.

I was shown that Mother-Father God places the Book of Gnosis (Knowledge) very safely and firmly within the divine feminine's heart, as Mother-Father God has decreed the divine feminine to be a living, multi-dimensional portal. This is in the sense that she has been governed with the ability to bring souls forth from the unseen realms into the seen realm.

Because she has been granted this extraordinary spiritual gift, this puts the divine feminine in the role of Mother; the one that carries the mother energy.

The mother energy in its healthy form is all about being in service at all times, to all souls. I was shown that Mother-Father God places the Book of Gnosis (Knowledge) firmly in the etheric field, or the heart space of the divine feminine.

If she has signed up to experience the full Ascension of her consciousness in this lifetime, then she will at some point be triggered to fully awaken. When she fully awakens, she will align with all of the codes of remembrance of the truth that she promised her divine masculine that she would awaken, through the purification of her egoic consciousness via the portal of her heart, and that she would remember that she is a divine feminine daughter of God.

I was shown in the vast majority of cases that it was the divine feminine who promised that she would awaken first and, in her awakening, she would connect spiritually and telepathically with her Twin Flame, the divine masculine, who is a conduit and a channel of spirit.

My Spirit team showed me that one of the most essential aspects of the Divine masculine's evolution is to ultimately surrender to the wisdom and the gnosis of the truly awakened divine feminine, and one of the most essential aspects of the Divine feminine's evolution is to be the spiritual protector for her divine masculine.

The divine feminine represents magnetism. I was shown that the divine masculine's ego must die and be reborn through the magnetism of the truly awakened, divine feminine.

The divine masculine holds the seed of the Christ-Self, firmly planted within him. But often, and in many cases, it is only when his true, divine feminine awakens to her eternal and perpetual divinity, as a daughter of Christ, or a feminine Christed being, that through her own perception and knowing she is able to recognise the Christ-Self that dwells in her divine masculine.

It is through her recognition of the Christ-Self in him; through her eyes and through her "perception" that the 'seed' of his Christ-Self, transforms into the 'fruit' of the Christed being that he has incarnated to be, whereby he then becomes one with his higher self.

There are so many dynamics at play when a divine masculine meets a truly awakened, divine feminine. She will never allow him to remain in a comatose state, nor will she allow him, on an energetic level, to stay in his comfort zone. She will be ever pushing him towards his self-realisation and full remembrance of his divinity. She will be a constant reminder to him that the third dimensional realm represents comfort, security, limitations and obligatory illusory karmic ties.

The divine masculine will very quickly realise that it is only when he truly surrenders to the divinity codes within his own being, and (once and for all) parents his terrified, abandoned, little boy self, that he will be able to stand as an equal match to the truly awakened, divine feminine.

It is a very rare man who is able to fully surrender to a truly awakened divine feminine, due to there being a limited number of divine feminines that are truly awakened on the third dimension. However, this is changing every single day.

If a divine masculine has attracted a truly awakened, divine feminine into his field, he must realise that, on a soul level, he has chosen this meeting and he is deeply ready for this alignment. He will also see that all of his previous relationships have been stepping-stones leading him to this ultimate surrender.

Twin Flames in The Tarot

One day it became apparent to me that there is so much spiritual truth depicted in the Tarot.

In the Tarot we can observe that the Fool represents the zero-point field of consciousness. The zero-point field is the space in which all souls are born and die. Zero in the Tarot represents the Fool and the beginning of the Fool's journey.

The first card in the Tarot deck is the Magician. Here we are shown a divine masculine holding a staff pointing up to the sky, which is symbolic of the fact that the divine masculine has incarnated to be a true living pillar of light and a conduit of divinity.

The second card in the Tarot is the High Priestess and here we see the High Priestess sitting on a throne, holding The Book of Gnosis (Knowledge). This is symbolic of the fact that Mother-Father God has bestowed upon the divine feminine access to the truth of the nature of reality, through the portal of her heart consciousness. This is because the divine feminine has been deemed less corruptible than the divine masculine, due to the fact that she is the Mother and is the chosen portal for souls entering into the earthly plane.

This myth is depicted throughout most ancient cultures that have held on to this knowing and remembrance, that the divine masculine is truly born when he surrenders and allows his egoic consciousness to die, to be reborn through the guidance, love, and abiding wisdom of the truly awakened, divine feminine.

The rewards for the divine masculine who is brave enough to face a truly awakened, divine feminine are impossible to express in human language. For the rewards are of the soul and are deeply connected to the expansion of one's soul consciousness and reaching a plateau of extraordinary alignment with one's higher self. This brings forth the experience of belonging, of homecoming and of knowing on the deepest level of your being, that your search is over.

Message for The Divine Masculine

Divine masculines, if you are reading these words, thank you so much for doing the work on yourself to align with the sacred message of this book and I ask you now to really set an intention to align with a truly awakened, divine feminine. One who has become one with her higher self and is truly an embodiment of the Goddess in human form. Trust me, they do exist. They are out there.

This is an invitation for you now to tune into your divine feminine and know that she is doing the work that she promised you that she would do; to truly awaken out of the nightmare of the third dimensional matrix. Know that she is working on herself to stabilise in higher dimensional consciousness and know that her motivation to do this, very often, is you.

Her love for you is her guiding force that is inspiring her to reach ever more deeply into the truth of who she truly is.

Please know that she thinks about you often and prays every day for your imminent alignment on the earthly dimension.

Divine masculines, if you are reading these words now, please take a moment to send a telepathic message of gratitude and love to your divine feminine. Tell her that you remember that you're both resting every night under the same stars and you are both looking up at the same moon.

It would be wise for you to send a prayer of gratitude to her for all the work that she is doing to prepare for your eternal union and to remind her that you are ready for her and that you trust that your meeting will align in divine timing.

Twin Flames and The Merkabah

The Merkabah has long been considered as a medium of Ascension. People have used its powers to raise their vibrations since ancient times.

The Merkabah is a combination of three different words:

Mer - is a light that rotates within itself

Ka - refers to the human spirit

Bah - refers to the physical human form

The Egyptians believed that the Merkabah is a rotating light that carries the human body and spirit from one plane to another.

When I experienced the Ascension of my consciousness in October 2013, I was shown that Twin Flames hold the identical Merkabah patterning. Essentially, God is a master Merkabah and we, as God's offspring, are fractals of that original Merkabah.

Prior to the Twins incarnation in separate vessels, each Twin Flame exists as one solid unit or Merkabah which then splits into two identical Twin Merkabic fields. One holding the masculine polarity and one holding the feminine polarity. Therefore, the Twin Flames truly hold identical vibratory resonances within their energetic signature. That is why the recognition of the Twin soul is so deep, abiding and unwavering.

I was shown that as we incarnate and descend from the higher dimensional realms into the lower dimensional earthly realm, our higher self stays ever connected to our Merkabic field like an umbilical cord. We each stay connected to our own Merkabah which is essentially the chariot that our soul resides in, as we traverse through this journey of experience; be that as a human earthly being, be that as a Pleiadian being, or be that as an Arcturian being.

A Merkabah is essentially a chariot of the spirit which carries you on your journey from the Godhead into the illusionary, yet somehow deeply entertaining experience of duality and separation. As we descend forth from the Godhead, we stay eternally connected to our Merkabah, which holds the identical pattern to our Twin soul.

The Times That We Are Living In

These truly are the most exciting times for any soul to be incarnated and please know that there is a very specific reason that you were chosen to be part of this planetary Ascension. On a galactic level, you have proven to have extremely important skills and tools that will help many, many of your brothers and sisters transition from third dimensional consciousness to fifth dimensional consciousness.

Please know there are many, many souls throughout the entire universe that are surrounding the earthly plane at the moment and who are watching closely this great show - this great Ascension show - as it unfolds.

It is so important for you to realise how precious you are, how important your specific role is in this planetary Ascension. Nothing is random. Without you, something very important would be missing from the whole. You hold an extremely important piece in this upcoming Ascension, and this is a sacred opportunity for you to accept that and remember your incredible divinity and amazing grace.

CHAPTER THREE - ZERO-POINT FIELD / 5D CONSCIOUSNESS

The Zero-point field is the present moment of now, and is the place that all duality merges into sacred Union.

There is a reason why I will devote much of this book to speaking about the Zero-point field and that is because your arrival and stabilisation in unity consciousness is intricately linked to the planet's Ascension.

When your consciousness arrives home at the Zero-point field, that is precisely what happens; you arrive home. The journey of searching and seeking comes to a final close. And all that you experience is the perpetual grace of resting in the deep, abiding knowing that you are home.

You are at the place where your soul has been seeking. You have arrived home at the place that you believed was an external place, but you remember that this could never be the case.

Our creator is so beautiful and benevolent. They would never, ever place the source of home, of happiness, of our wellbeing, of eternal peace, outside of ourselves. With love and abiding grace, it has been placed within our consciousness.

As with many deeply esoteric subjects when one speaks about the fifth dimension, it can seem somewhat ambiguous and mystical to many, so I would like to devote the next chapter to share with you what I've directly experienced about fifth-dimensional consciousness.

When you arrive home in the Zero-point field of consciousness, you realise that this is the gateway point to the fifth dimension. Before entering into the Zero-point field, you realise that your consciousness was previously hovering around the third-dimensional realm of consciousness and the fourth-dimensional realm.

Once you arrive truly at home within the present moment of now, this is when you arrive in the heart space, which is the fifth dimension.

The fifth dimension is the place of unity consciousness. It is the place where sacred union is the order of the day.

May we all be reminded here that fifth-dimensional consciousness is only accessed through love and via the portal of our imaginal faculties and truth of the heart.

It is the dimensional reality where all that exists is the divine and sacred marriage of you and your divine beloved.

Within the Zero-point field, all polarity and all duality ends. We still see the dance of polarity and duality within the fourth-dimensional realms of consciousness. It is only when we get to the fifth dimension that we truly transcend this entire dance of duality and we arrive home into the Zero-point field of divine sacred union - union with self, union with your beloved and union with God.

At this juncture, it would be appropriate to share with you that I have been shown that in the fifth-dimensional realms of consciousness, the masculine and feminine polarities of the Twin Flame still have a higher dimensional crystalline form, and so the dance of the polarity still takes place on some level. However, the notion of duality and separation has been entirely transcended on all levels of consciousness when one arrives home to the Zero-point field also known as fifth-dimensional consciousness.

In the moment of my awakening, I remembered that all timelines operate concurrently within the Zero-point field. Through my imagination, I can visit any timeline that my soul has or will ever experience through my attention and intention.

When one comes home to the Zero-point field/fifth-dimensional consciousness, there is a full reunion with the Akashic fields, connecting you to your own soul's evolutionary journey. Thus, many past lives and timelines that you have experienced are revealed to you, which have been stored eternally in the Zero-point field of consciousness.

One Person Stabilising in Fifth Dimensional Consciousness

The reason why one person's true stability in enlightened consciousness is so powerful and effective for the collective is that we are all essentially tuning forks. This means that when one of us attains a true and stabilised level of spiritual mastery, this in effect sends out a master tone on a vibrational level to the entire collective.

We are all one. We are all brothers and sisters. We are all the direct off-spring of Mother-Father God. We are all intricately and intimately connected on a subtle and energetic level. Therefore, when one person truly has attained spiritual enlightenment, it profoundly fast-tracks everybody else to come to that same vibratory frequency.

All is truly one. Every grain of sand, every flower, every child, every star, every galactic being, every human being is perfectly and intricately woven into the perfection of creation. Creation would not be the same if that grain of sand were not present. Creation would be lacking if that singular blade of grass were not present.

Everybody is intricately connected on a profound unconscious level. And as I mentioned earlier, in truth, individual identity is a construct of the lower dimensional realms of consciousness. As we attain the higher levels of consciousness, all individuality ceases to exist and our consciousness returns ever closer to the perpetual truth of God's grace.

Be as a child, trusting in knowing that you are eternally safe; you are loved, and you are protected. The thoughts that are running through your mind are often not even your thoughts and can be likened to streams of matrix information, flowing in the collective. We all absorb these and they're usually not personal to us, even though they appear to be. This is why it is so essential for us to be the observer of the monkey mind (the egoic consciousness).

The fifth dimension is the gateway point to the Zero-point field, which is unity consciousness, the truth that exists beyond duality.

Beyond the fourth dimension is the fifth dimension, the realm where you and your eternal Twin Flame dance in perpetual bliss throughout all the higher dimensional realms of consciousness. In the fifth dimension, you are in perpetual union with your Twin Flame and your union is eternally sealed in God's deepest grace.

Vibrationally you are linked from the fifth dimension above to your androgynous soul unit, soul signature pattern, which is identical in nature to your Twin Flame and is a living fractal of God.

In my awakening, spirit showed me that the fifth-dimensional sacred union between Twin Flames is eternally activated and harmonious, and it is our job as awakened avatar beings to attune to the fifth-dimensional realms of consciousness and the rapturous bliss that resides there.

Words Are Spells

The purpose of this book is to remind you that you are automatically plugged into the higher mind of God-consciousness through you actively choosing higher thoughts. Thoughts of service, thoughts of gratitude, thoughts whereby you are counting your blessings, and of course the practice of committing deeply to meeting and bringing home your shadow self.

There is a current that exists, that is known as the force of creation. This force holds all the stars in their place and is what transforms a seed into a flower.

It is our job as individualised transmitters to attune to this blissful and extraordinary current. We do that through attuning or indeed choosing our thoughts and remembering in every moment that we are empowered to place our extremely powerful consciousness wherever it is that we intend.

When one has truly arrived home in fifth-dimensional consciousness, one takes full responsibility for all of the thoughts and spells that are cast out of one's being. One remembers that one is a creator being and therefore, almighty in terms of one's creative powers.

One consequently remembers that it is our duty and responsibility to be eternally vigilant regarding that which is being sent out into the universe, consciously through thoughts and through the spoken word.

The fifth-dimensional realm is a self-sovereign, self-aligned state of being where we are granted the ability to choose - every moment of every day.

One who is fully anchored in fifth dimensional consciousness remembers to create one's reality using one's imaginal faculties, and remembers one is infinitely empowered to do so at all times.

If you are committed to purging all of the false programming which has enforced the idea of lack into your sacred consciousness, and if you have returned home to the truth that you are an innocent child of God, then please know this is truly the most important work your soul can do in this lifetime.

We must fully claim our remembrance and our true knowing, that wherever we focus our attention and intention is exactly what we will be calling into our reality to experience as a direct manifestation.

In our fully awakened state, we remember that we are individualised radio transmitters and it is our cosmic duty to attune to higher dimensional thoughts of empowerment and creatorship.

When we do this we transcend the matrix's constant obsession to pull us into the notion that we are a victim of this realm - when nothing could be further from the truth.

This entire book is a coaching call of the highest order

Essentially this entire book is a coaching call of the highest order, blasting through the sticky veils of the lower dimensions and piercing you right back in the centre of your hearts, knowing and remembering that you are a precious divine child of God.

The world has sought to deny you that, but the truth will forever be the truth. Your divinity is ingrained in creation; your divinity is undeniable to all who have eyes that can truly see and which have been untainted by the false dark programming of the lower dimensional matrix.

For us to access the Kingdom and Queendom of God, we must become like children again - truthful, authentic and unfiltered. We must commit to becoming empty vessels and every day make the conscious choice to orientate our thoughts and actions towards that which is positive, remembering that we are all individualised transmitters, and the thoughts that we choose are how we attune with the universal song of creation.

We Are All Fractals of God

Mother-Father God is a vast and expansive realm of diamond crystalline consciousness and we are each fragments of that diamond crystalline consciousness.

In many ways, the truth is that our individual identity does not even exist in the true nature of reality, as there is absolutely nothing that can ever be separate from God.

It would be extremely accurate to say that our individual identity is a dream. Our individual identity is a creational, temporary construct, which sprang forth from the heart of the ovoid oneness of God/creation, for the sole purpose of having the experience of polarity and duality, that these experiences could be added to the infinity of God's expansive creational template.

This ensures that we continually keep experiencing the ecstatic, blissful and rapturous reunion of self-reuniting with self on each sojourn the soul goes on, in its perceived separation from source energy.

It is our sacred duty to remember that separation is a construct of the third dimension and is also rife within the fourth-dimensional realms of consciousness.

The more our consciousness attunes to the higher echelons of the fifth-dimensional realms it becomes glaringly apparent that the entire notion of separation is a lie.

All that exists is the ecstatic union and celebration of creation unifying with itself. This is the true template of creation, and everything else, which is temporary, is not recorded within the Halls of Amenti (the great halls of creation) for only love is eternal. And if it is not love, it is not true and it does not exist except in the realm of illusion. All that gets stored in the sacred records of creation is the truth.

Therefore, please accept this invitation to drop the egoic obsession in believing that you have an important identity, that you are separate from your Brothers and Sisters and that you are unsafe in this realm of creation.

These words here are an invitation for you to entirely let go of all of the programming of the third dimension, which has sought to keep you entrapped in this Samsaric realm of repetition and perpetual stagnation.

If these words resonate with you, please know that this message is streaming forth directly from your higher self, who is communicating to you, this message.

Do you want to know how to make Mother-Father God do a happy dance? You, relaxing at this moment, dropping all your worries, all your burdens, all your fears, all your projections and allowing yourself to drop into your heart space like you are on holiday, like you are on vacation.

Every time we can drop our thoughts, cares and worries and allow ourselves to rest in a moment of relaxation, we make Mother-Father God do an exceptionally wonderful, happy dance.

Who I am is an Eternal Child of God

It would serve us well to remember that society, this third-dimensional matrix, will never give us permission to be who we truly are. Therefore, it is our duty and responsibility to step forward as sovereign beings and take our own crown from the etheric plane and place it very intentionally and very steadily upon our own head so that it may be worn with great radiance, humility and the deepest desire to serve all of our Brothers and Sisters at all times.

Through us wearing our sacred crown without shame, our Brothers and Sisters will remember that Mother-Father God also placed a crown in their etheric field, and it is their sacred duty and responsibility to take it out of the etheric realm and place it securely on their head.

Another considerable part of the illusion of the third dimension is that you have to jump through hoops and have master's degrees and receive all manner of certificates to be who you truly are. When really the truth is - you are a child of the universe - a sovereign being of the highest order - an off-spring of Mother-Father God; a creator being of the highest order. Your spiritual authority is self-ordained and is a part of your birthright.

You promised your Brothers and Sisters that you would remember your sovereignty, that you are a Son or a Daughter of Mother-Father God. You promised that you would wear your crown with pride, so that all of your Brothers and Sisters may recognise their own perpetual and eternal divinity through your remembrance.

This is the duty of all the 144,000 Twin Flame Starseed divine pairs! We incarnated, promising that we would remember that we are sovereign and there is no one above us and there is no one below us.

We are each children of God and our spiritual authority must be self-ordained.

That one sentence is the true golden key to enlightenment because what holds back so many on the spiritual path is the waiting for external validation from a being that you perceive as spiritually superior to you, be that a human being or an ascended master. It is very often this mindset that keeps everybody entrapped in the lower dimensional Samsaric realms.

You are seeking the peace and tranquility of the divine spark of truth that you are. This spark does not exist outside of yourself, for Mother-Father God would only place this spark within you. Therefore, you can rest deeply in the knowledge that all that you seek, resides within you.

The moment you stop this external search and take the reins back from your egoic consciousness, you start dedicating your thoughts towards an orientation of positivity and celebration. It is then that you will experience a genuine shift in your reality, thus activating all of the spiritual mastery codes that are stored within your DNA.

This Book is Full of Codes

This book is full of codes streaming forth directly from the heart of the core of existence and we are all deeply connected to that heart-field. In receiving these words, you will experience a beautiful and profound opening or indeed flowering of your DNA patterning. Triggering those so-called junk DNA strands to quickly align and rearrange themselves in the 12-strand diamond configuration pattern which was tampered with at the time of the fall of Atlantis.

My deepest intention is that the words of this book quickly snap you back into the remembrance that you are the stabilised lighthouses that you promised all your Brothers and Sisters that you would be; that you have fully remembered your sacred promise to be the one to hold and reflect the light of everyone's true divine multi-dimensionality.

Faith Codes and Imagination

In this book, every word is specifically directed to support you to very quickly and swiftly align with the spiritual master, Avatar being, that you truly are. The galactic, angelic, timeless, off-spring of eternal love.

An essential step in truly stabilising as a spiritual master is to have unwavering faith in the unseen realm. We choose to remember that we are multi-dimensional beings, having a third-dimensional Earth-based experience, and we remember that it does take a little bit of time for the visions that have been set forth on the higher planes of existence to manifest and anchor on the lower earthly dimensional planes of reality.

This is where so many Starseeds get frustrated, which is why it can often take so long to manifest our heart's desires. It is absolutely and purely about faith, so therefore, please accept this invitation now to realise that faith is a choice.

You will never arrive at the plateau of faith because life was easy and great. On the contrary, life will show you the opposite of that, as the litmus test to see where you stand on the faith spectrum.

Therefore, please accept this invitation to fully step onto the path of faith; right here, right now in the present moment. Have faith that it is not random that you have been drawn to these sacred words. It is not random that your higher self has led you to these words.

This is an invitation for you to have faith in God, faith that you are one of the 144,000 Starseed Twin Flames, whose divine sacred union was seeded at the time of Lemuria. This is an invitation for you to have faith in your divine beloved, your eternal divine consort, the one who holds the identical energetic and vibrational signature to you. This is an invitation to know that your union will manifest in perfect divine timing and be unlike any other relationship you have ever experienced.

We live in such a beautiful, vast and benevolent universe, and we are all naturally attuned to be high vibrational beings. Yet, life on planet Earth - or in the third dimension - has sought to create as many distortions as possible between us and our naturally high vibration. Therefore the importance of faith cannot be reiterated enough on this journey.

Please take this as a sacred reminder that you will only manifest what you believe already exists on the unseen planes. If you are waiting to see something first, to believe that it is real, then you will be waiting for a very long time.

It would serve us all well to remember that we live in a thought universe and our imagination is directly linked to the mind of God.

Every time we hold a vision - a knowing in our imagination - we effectively release that program into the universal matrix, with clear instructions for this to manifest in as swift and efficient a manner as possible.

However, if one sends out a visualisation to the universe and then starts looking for reasons and excuses to come to the conclusion that it has not manifested or it is not manifesting, then in effect, this is collapsing that visualisation instruction within the universal matrix field. This then sends forth information to the universe to stop pursuing this particular visualisation instruction.

Therefore, it is absolutely imperative if you are to get the most from this book that you commit now to a path of unwavering faith; unwavering faith in yourself, in Mother-Father God, the universe and your divine, beloved Twin Flame.

You have absolutely everything you need within you to manifest this union. Indeed, this union is encoded in the deepest aspect of your DNA and all of your cells and molecules. It is very, very difficult to mess this up – but not impossible. The quickest way to mess this up is to doubt your inner-knowing and become critical around the speed in which your visualisations are manifesting.

Dearest one, you are invited now to take this moment to choose to have faith.

Billions of books have been created in the world and you were drawn to this book for a reason. Your higher self has brought you to this book and that is because it contains codes that are specifically connected to you and your evolutionary journey toward spiritual mastery.

This is also known as the eternal remembrance of your perpetual innocence as a child of God.

Law of Attraction

This book would not be complete unless I spoke about the Law of Attraction from a spiritual perspective.

A considerable part of the programming of the third dimension is the false belief that our power is accessed through placing our awareness on 'what is occurring' as opposed to remembering that it is our sacred duty and responsibility to choose and attune to that which we, as Godly beings, wish to experience.

That is probably the number one spell that has been cast upon God's beautiful, sweet, children of the light.

We must awaken from this spell immediately, and use the power of our God-given imagination to place our awareness and somatic experience on the Direct knowing that we are manifesting whatever it is that we wish to manifest - regardless of what is being presented to us on the third dimensional realm.

When this is fully understood, one has a breakthrough and becomes a master manifestor.

One of the most important aspects of working with the Law of Attraction is to become extremely mindful and vigilant over the words that we speak, as they are the spells that we cast.

If you can become hyper-vigilant about the words that you speak and make sure to not put out negative spells continuously, this one act will cause a massive shift in your spiritual vibration and your relationship with the Law of Attraction.

Please see my chapter on the Law of Attraction in my workbook that goes with this book. There is a very powerful exercise and meditation that will enhance your relationship with the law of attraction miraculously.

The Law of Attraction works best when we play with it with the spirit of the eternal child. It is very powerful to find Law of Attraction playmates whom you can work together with to script future timelines. What is recommended is speaking as though the timeline that you wish to experience has already manifested in the way that you intend it to.

This is called scripting and is a potent tool for manifesting. I also recommend working with vision boards and any visual aids to support your subconscious mind to manifest your heart's desire, very swiftly and efficiently.

I also highly recommend reading my small book titled "The Law of Attraction - Little Instruction Book." It is packed from cover to cover with extremely potent quotes which are in effect tools to help you work with the Law of Attraction in the most extraordinary way.

Since birthing that book, my abundance levels have increased ten times, and I can always manifest everything I want, whenever I want it.

Very soon, Beloveds, I will talk about the fastest way to attain spiritual enlightenment. I will share with you phenomenal practices that will enable you to fully stabilise in fifth-dimensional consciousness, also known as enlightened consciousness.

CHAPTER FOUR - SPIRITUAL MASTERY

No matter how far you get on the path of spiritual enlightenment, you can never get rid of your thoughts or your ego. Just like the sky can never eliminate the clouds. The sky always remembers that it is eternal, it is presence, it is empty and it is the space in which all matter, all phenomena, is allowed to rise and fall, be that hurricanes or be that rainbows.

Our consciousness is just like that. We are like the sky – vast, empty, expansive and able to hold space for all appearances. Our thoughts are like clouds; they are temporary and they come and go. They look real, but they only ever remain in the temporal realms.

I have trained myself to view my thoughts as I would an awful radio station, playing in the background, which I am under no obligation to tune in and listen to.

Spiritual Mastery Practice Number 1 - Becoming an Empty Channel

A fundamental part of spiritual mastery is becoming empty. All instruments are empty. A guitar is empty, a drum is empty, a flute is empty. An instrument must be empty so that it can be filled with the light and the grace of the divine.

I remember very clearly sitting at the feet of Mother-Father-God, making a promise that I would devote my time on Earth to being an empty vessel. I also remember

Mother-Father-God promising me that in that exact moment of attaining emptiness, the light of the highest divine grace would enter my being.

The spiritual practice that I'm about to share with you brings you to that place of emptiness and can be considered the Maha spiritual practice on the path to enlightenment.

Our higher self knows it is not ever our job to work out the *how's* of manifesting anything in the universe. It is simply our job to become empty channels, empty vessels, so that the flow of the divine Christed light of creation may enter us, so we may be filled with the eternal and perpetual light of God's love.

Therefore, may these words trigger your DNA. May these words trigger deep soul remembrances within you, that there is no saviour. There is no Messiah. There is no Twin Flame and there is no guru that could possibly save you. You are your own master and the choices you make either free you or make you a slave.

Right now, you can decide to choose the path of making proactive choices towards positive thinking and positively showing up as a force of great good in the world; or you can choose to be perpetually run by your unconscious ego, which seeks to be extremely self-obsessed, narcissistic and entirely forgetful of the memo that we have each incarnated into this realm to help and serve one another.

This 3D matrix is probably the most challenging place for the soul to ever incarnate. And in our empowerment and our Remembrance we remember that everyone on Earth is experiencing trauma or PTSD to some degree or another.

We remember that it is our duty to show up as the benevolent forces of positivity, kindness and divine presence in every opportunity we are presented with; that we may be the vibration of home, of calm, of resting, to all of those who are blessed to come and bask in our sacred presence.

Spiritual Mastery Practice Number 2 – Observe The Monkey Mind

This conjecture would be a perfect time to share with you all a spiritual practice that has been truly life-changing for me.

It is prevalent on the spiritual path to believe that you are searching for Something outside of yourself in order to attain enlightenment. However, this programme is a massive linchpin of the third dimension and has held everyone back on their Ascension path and is one of the greatest lies ever to be told.

One of the most life-changing realisations for me was when I realised that all of us have only ever been searching for ourselves.

That self, also known as the Atman, is the eternal self that resides within all of God's creations and can only ever be accessed through the present moment of now.

When you attain mastery over the egoic consciousness (the monkey mind) through a dedicated spiritual practice and through orienting your thoughts towards that which you are grateful for. As soon as you make these fundamental shifts and choices within your daily routine, you will be utterly amazed at how quickly you align with the true benevolent force of creation, which is in and of itself an incredibly joyful, blissful and ecstatic vibration.

If repeated over and over in this book it would serve us all well to remember that essentially, we are all radio transmitters and it is our responsibility to attune to the remembrance that in every single moment we are empowered to make conscious choices.

In fact, is our duty to attune to the reality that we wish to experience. We do this despite the incessantly negative narrative of our egoic consciousness that is perpetually addicted to being a victim and believing that it is an individualised drop of water, separated from the ocean of existence.

The egoic consciousness is ever-vigilant in its attempt to lure you into the false belief of separation. And therefore, to attain any steps forward on your spiritual path, you must commit to a disciplined spiritual practice.

This is the only way you will be able to work with your ego's incessant energy, which is perpetually seeking to pull you away into thoughts of the past and fearful thoughts of the future.

My most sincere hope is that you truly awaken to the remembrance that what your soul has always been seeking is not external from yourself. It is you and this is accessed through your choice to relax and rest in this eternal present moment of now.

As we arrive in the present moment, also known as the Zero-point field, we quickly realise that the egoic monkey mind is on a mission 100% of the time to pull us away from the present moment, through incessant thoughts of the past and the future.

It becomes glaringly apparent that the ego's job is to keep you away from the glory of the present moment. And so, in a cosmic nutshell, without a spiritual practice, you will find it very challenging to stabilise in higher consciousness.

Please know that there are very powerful exercises and techniques in the accompanying workbook that go along with this book which will help you very deeply stabilise in the Zero-point field.

The True Nature of Self

I believe the sky is the greatest analogy to explain the true nature of consciousness. The sky can be likened to the true self; it is eternal, expansive, wide, vast and empty, and able to hold space for all temporary meteorological appearances.

And this is the truth of your consciousness - you are eternal grace manifested in physical form, and part of your soul contract is to be a receiver of collective thought streams.

Just as the sky holds space for hurricanes, tornadoes, heavy rain and drought whilst never forgetting that it is indeed the pure empty, pristine sky, when we incarnate into this earthly matrix, we sign up to be the receivers of collective thought streams within the matrix.

Ultimately, if we are on the awakening Ascension path, we have a great opportunity to use these afflictive thought forms to wake us up to the true nature of reality.

This is done through the simple yet extremely powerful act of being the observer of one's thoughts, as opposed to believing every thought we think and identifying with them.

There is never a moment where the sky forgets its eternal glory and identifies as a temporary cloud. Just as we must never identify with the limited, fear-based, incessant narrative of the egoic consciousness, if you "commit" to the spiritual practices I will shortly speak about in this book, you will more than likely attain enlightenment.

The sky never forgets that it is the sky and this is the truth of each of our soul journeys, to awaken and remember the eternal truth that:

I Am that I Am - Pure Sky Consciousness.

A great affirmation to repeat would be:

I am pure emptiness. I am pure grace. I am the space in which all phenomena has a permission space to rise and fall.

I Am that I Am.

I am the observer.

I have transcended the need to identify with the temporary appearances of thought-forms, just as the sky remains empty and neutral to the display of all manner of weather phenomena.

Resting as Consciousness for Short Moments

I would like to take this opportunity to share with you a potent spiritual practice that I have been working with since 2012.

This is a profound, ancient Buddhist practice taught to many, many monks in the Himalayas for thousands of years.

I was fortunate and blessed to have met a modern-day Buddhist teacher in India, in Goa, in 2012. There, I took part in a training called the Twelve Empowerments.

Participating in the Twelve Empowerments, I embarked on a "training" programme to train myself to rest as awareness for short moments.

The practice is to simply, in this moment, stop thinking, jump off the thought train and bring one's awareness to the present moment. To feel the carpet under our toes; observe the wallpaper on the wall, whatever it takes, to focus our awareness on the present moment.

And we do that by choosing to literally jump off the thought train.

Every single time we choose to take a short moment and rest as awareness, in effect, we are communicating to our egoic consciousness that it is no longer in control. We are showing that incessant aspect of ourself that I, the divine presence within, am now in control, and am guiding and directing my consciousness in this moment to drop into presence, stillness and awareness.

The teacher that I worked with always used to say to us, “It may not seem like the most significant thing in the world taking a short moment, but visualise it like this: Every time you choose to take a short moment, in effect, you are taking a pearl and you are placing it on a string.”

At the end of the day, if you have remembered to take many short moments, you will have an entire necklace of pearls. These pearls represent clarity, a clarity that does not come from the mind. They represent a clarity and a knowing that comes from the deepest self, the deepest part of your being.

In effect, what I am speaking about here is a training programme that trains you to turn down the volume of the constant, repetitive, victim-obsessed voice of your egoic consciousness and encourages you to empower your intuitive knowing and helps you access the deepest level of gnosis that exists within you.

Enlightenment is not for the lazy. You will never attain enlightenment if you give up or take a break or decide to have a rest for a day. The very nature of the egoic mind is to pull you away from the present, into thoughts of fear and worry. Therefore, to attain spiritual enlightenment, unwavering commitment to this must mean everything to you.

This must be the number one priority in your life. You must commit deeply and avidly to attaining spiritual enlightenment and then pursue this through a dedicated and committed spiritual practice. I have been committed to this spiritual practice since 2012, and due to this practice's potency, I went on to experience the Ascension of my consciousness in 2013.

I know without a shadow of a doubt if I had not committed to this practice, I would not have experienced the Ascension of my consciousness.

The Practice

So, let's do it now... The practice: For one moment, just stop thinking. Bring your awareness to the present moment. Feel the carpet under your toes and look at the colour of the wallpaper. Of course, your thoughts will come back two seconds later. That is the very nature of thoughts. But that's it! That's all you have to do, whenever you naturally remember to do so. Jump off the thought train and bring your awareness to the present moment.

The more times in the day that you remember to do that, the quicker you will attain spiritual enlightenment.

There are indeed no words that can adequately express how powerful this spiritual practice is. And it is my deep and sincere prayer that everybody reading these words commit to a spiritual practice such as this, which will help you attain full spiritual mastery in this lifetime.

Please see the chapter in my accompanying workbook, which speaks in greater depth about this spiritual practice and shares more exercises and tools to be able to assist you to commit to this practice.

As soon as you commit to this practice, you will observe that you very quickly align with the true vibration of creation which is, in and of itself, benevolent and extremely blissful.

***Become Mindful of Your Words*.**

In order to become a spiritual master, you have to be very, very vigilant with the language that you use. Every time you speak, you are a creator. You are creating that reality.

Please know that this is an invitation for you, from this moment on, to become very mindful about **THE WORDS** that you speak.

This is a sacred invitation for you to cease your addiction to talking negatively about anything in your life, especially yourself.

To be a spiritual master, you have to cut negativity at its root. You have to say, "From this day on, I'm not going to be a victim. I'm not going to share my victim story with the world. From now on, I am not going to say, to the whole world: 'this happened to me and that happened to me' because that's just my story."

The true spiritual master decides to let their story go, in order to be empty, because they remember their promise to Mother-Father God to be empty, just like a guitar, a glute, and a drum.

We've all got a story. You've got a sob story - I've got a sob story. The whole world has got a sob story, but that story is not going to take you to the fifth dimension. The only way that you're going to get to the fifth dimension is by being strong and powerful, and putting down that story and promising to never, ever pick it up again.

When I put this into practice my vibrational level transformed so quickly and I stabilised in fifth dimensional consciousness almost immediately. I realised it was my addiction to speaking about my story that was keeping my vibration very, very stuck and very, very low.

In effect I was taking that empty instrument that I truly am, and stuffing it with rags (old beliefs) so that it could not be played properly.

When I realised this in 2011, it hit me like a thunderbolt. I realised that I had been scripting everything that I didn't want to happen my whole life. I realised I was addicted to proving to everyone in my life, as well as God,- the universe, that I was a victim and that nothing ever worked out for me.

I quickly realised that this was a profound affliction and addiction that I had been attached to for many, many years. I realised that this was also the case for all my Brothers and Sisters (unless you are completely enlightened).

I realised that a huge part of the programming of the third dimension is a constant attachment to the notion that I am a victim, that life is very, very difficult, and here is the evidence that shows you that I am right.

It was only when I had that significant lightbulb moment in 2011 after watching a show on YouTube about the people who created the "The Secret" that I was deeply struck by the realisation that I would never, ever do that again. I would never, ever speak in a way that would be creating my life to be anything other than my highest joy and my highest destiny.

From that moment on, I committed to taking full responsibility for every word that I spoke. I stopped talking about my life from the perspective of what it currently looked like and I began speaking into existence that which I wished to manifest.

I have been fortunate and very blessed in my life to experience several powerful spiritual breakthroughs and this was definitely one of them. I quickly noticed that as soon as you make that adjustment regarding your thoughts and begin orienting them towards the positive, you very quickly align with the benevolent vibration of creation. This force holds the stars in their places and transforms an egg and a sperm into a baby.

There is an energy, a stream of consciousness, that is all God and all good. We as human transmitters have a duty and a responsibility to attune our consciousness to this higher frequency band.

To attune ourselves with this eternal and perpetual vibration of creation; one of the primary and fundamental ways we do this is to cease our addiction to perpetually spewing forth our "poor me" story to any soul who comes into our vicinity.

I really cannot express how quickly the shift happens once you commit to cease the addiction to speaking about your 'story' incessantly, particularly from the vibration of being a victim or from being in any way identified with that story, i.e., that you are who you are because of what happened to you.

Rampages of Gratitude

I would like to introduce another extremely powerful and life-changing spiritual practice that has changed my life, and that is committing to the practice of gratitude. The importance of committing to the spiritual practice of gratitude cannot be over-emphasised. I mentioned earlier in this book that I had a life-changing epiphany when I watched many of the speakers who appeared in the famous documentary film "The Secret."

After watching this documentary, it dawned on me that I had been co-creating everything that I didn't want to happen in my life to actually happen.

I realised that I was not taking responsibility for the thoughts that were allowed a complete free rein, in my divine consciousness.

I realised that unless I committed to the path of choosing to direct my thoughts in alignment with that which is uplifting and beneficial, I would carry on having the unsatisfying life that I was living. And thus, I would keep on experiencing all that I wished to not experience.

This was such a life-changing epiphany for me, as I genuinely had not realised that I could have control over the ongoing egoic narrative that was perpetually running in my consciousness.

As I watched these inspirational speakers talk, I was inspired to fully commit to the path of gratitude.

I made a promise to myself that from that moment on, I would imagine that in my consciousness there existed a Tiger ready to pounce on any negative thought that slipped out of my mind.

I learned the practice of becoming vigilant and mindful of the thoughts that I was thinking and I learned an incredible technique that if, for example, a negative thought or a worrying thought slipped out by accident, I could repeat the word "cancel" to cancel that thought from attracting energy in the universe that would turn it into a physical reality.

There are no words that can adequately express how much my life changed when I committed to this practice and my vibration went from being medium-high to absolutely off the charts.

At this time, I was incredibly inspired and empowered to create a small pocketbook titled "The Law of Attraction - Little Instruction Book." I had a very clear vision to create the book which would be comprised of many well-known people speaking about the Law of Attraction.

I had a very clear vision of the book and I set myself four weeks to create it and have the hard copy in my hand.

I manifested it in the time frame that I intended to, and it was an incredibly life-changing experience for me. Still to this day, this is my go-to book if ever I have a wobble, which is very rare since I stabilised in fifth dimensional consciousness.

However, on the odd occasion I do have a little emotional wobble, the first thing I do is reach for my "Law of Attraction - Little Instruction Book." It is, without doubt, the most powerful book I've ever held in my hands.

There is something so potent and so magical in this book's alchemy that automatically brings the reader back to alignment with their higher self. Please see the back of this book on how to order this powerful life-changing little book.

I was no longer stuck in a quagmire of fear and worry, which was perpetually pointing out problems and pitfalls. Instead, I was directing my consciousness to focus on that which I am grateful for.

This massively affected my spiritual vibration. My vibration increased very quickly, which resulted in me experiencing and receiving many downloads about the true nature of reality and manifestation.

I have been shown that creation co-exists on a particular frequency band. There is a force in the universe that creates flowers, trees, stars, planets, babies, animals - the works.

I realised that this force was extraordinarily benevolent in nature, and it is our job as human radio transmitters to take control and responsibility of our egoic consciousness, so that we can adjust our own individual transmitters to be in alignment with this benevolent frequency of creation.

I realised very quickly that the force of goodness in the universe is all-powerful, and as soon as we commit to adjusting our thoughts to a more positive vibration, then it is almost instantly that we come into alignment with this benevolent energetic frequency of creation and thus the experience of greater fortune and instant miracles.

I noticed that when this happens, when our individual vibration comes into alignment with the benevolent force of creation, this means that we massively shift old, third-dimensional timelines and, as though we are on a trampoline, we jump to higher timelines.

We get to experience fortuitous meetings of destiny, synchronicities, the experience of our abundance codes being activated, and so much more.

I believe the spiritual practice of gratitude is so powerful and so important for all of those who wish to stabilise in enlightened consciousness.

Before having a spiritual practice such as this, one's egoic consciousness is allowed to entirely run the show. In many ways the egoic consciousness can be likened to a blind person who has been given the enormous responsibility of being in the driver's seat of your life, but who has absolutely no connection to the overall journey that you are going on. It can only deal with a minimal-width band of information, unlike the heart consciousness which is akin to a GPS, which knows the quickest, fastest and most efficient route to all destinations, including your highest spiritual destiny.

The satellite GPS is the most accurate analogy which explains the heart consciousness, where the blueprint of our greatest spiritual destiny is held.

When we attune to our heart and follow the guidance that we receive, we know that we are on the fastest and quickest route towards our destiny.

The egoic consciousness is only able to view what is directly ahead of it. In contrast, the heart consciousness is plugged into every other super consciousness in existence, and is intricately connected to all information that is simply not available to the conscious mind.

So, until one commits to a spiritual practice of gratitude, we are governed by our egoic consciousness, which genuinely has no clue how to get anyone to the fifth dimension.

In my upcoming workbook I speak in depth about gratitude and I share tools and exercises that help you commit deeply to this incredibly life-changing spiritual practice.

As soon as we commit to the practice of gratitude, we are glitching the egoic matrix and informing it that it is no longer in control. Our heart consciousness, our higher self, is now taking back the reins, through the fact that we are taking responsibility and directing our consciousness towards thoughts that are uplifting and directing them towards thoughts of gratitude.

If there's one thing that you take from this book, I hope it is this: that you commit to a path of gratitude and resting as awareness as a spiritual practice.

May you commit to the practice of going on endless barrages of gratitude, whether you're doing the washing up or driving to collect your children or walking to the post office. Instead of just using that time to worry about all the terrible things that could go wrong in your life, this is an invitation for you to use that precious time to become obsessed with being grateful.

Be grateful for your fingers and your toes. Be grateful that you have eyes to see and ears to hear. Be grateful for the blue sky above you and be grateful for the beautiful Robin Redbreasts singing their morning song as the sun rises.

Be grateful for the dew on the grass and be grateful for the mighty mama ocean. Be grateful for your children. Be grateful for your parents. Be grateful for all of the gifts that you take for granted. Be grateful for a warm bed to sleep in. Be grateful for this book in your hands. Be grateful for the hot drink that you will have later. There are so many things for us all to be grateful for.

This is a potent spiritual practice that will change your life if you commit to it.

I hope I've explained why choosing the path of gratitude is so powerful spiritually. In a nutshell, as we orient our thoughts towards that which is benevolent and positive, we're automatically aligning with the benevolent force of creation - the force that creates absolutely everything. When we, as transmitters and receivers, align with this energetic frequency, this is when we truly align on the path of our greatest spiritual destiny.

All of the universe is uplifting, loving and of a high vibration. It is only the lower dimensional realms that have been hijacked through the galactic wars and the Earth's quarantine, which have enforced onto the collective a false matrix programme which says that struggle and strife are a natural part of one's evolutionary journey.

However, this is an illusion and is part of the false third dimensional matrix.

May all of you who are reading these words remember that one of the most powerful and potent ways to get out of the matrix is by redirecting and orienting our thoughts towards that which we are grateful for.

When you commit to a spiritual practice of attuning yourself and reminding yourself to be grateful for all of the blessings that you have in your reality - be that the fact that you have eyes to see - ears to hear - a family that loves you - a roof over your head - the fact that you live in a world where the birds are singing… As soon as you make those choices to attune to those positive thoughts, you very, very quickly align with the highest and most benevolent vibrations of creation and you start attracting synchronicities, divine meetings and fortuitous moments of destiny.

These two practices of resting as awareness for short moments and endlessly going on barrages of gratitude work together so beautifully and I have found that mixing up these practices makes life powerful and transformative.

In order to experience shifts in your reality, it is essential that you commit to a spiritual practice; dipping your toes in for a day or two will get you nowhere. My recommendation is that you commit to a spiritual practice for the rest of your life and then watch how quickly you stabilise in enlightened consciousness.

When you commit to choosing to focus on thoughts of gratitude and all the ways that you can serve your Brothers and Sisters, be they large or small, then it is merely a matter of cosmic seconds until your soul frequency aligns with the exquisite vibration of creation.

The fact that you are reading these words has inspired me to set you a challenge to go forth and do this: From this moment on, give up your addiction to telling your sob story to as many people as possible and instead go on rampages of gratitude ceaselessly and endlessly throughout your day, then please report back how your life has transformed in one week from now.

Reminder to Rest in this Moment

Throughout this book, I will keep on repeating to you to rest for a moment. If you are serious about committing to this spiritual practice, I would highly recommend having yellow Post-it notes around your house reminding you to rest for a moment. Indeed, you could take it a step further and create beautiful artwork that reminds you to rest for a short moment.

I would like to take this opportunity to express my deepest and sincerest gratitude to the organisation that is called Balanced View, under the excellent teacher Candice O'Denver.

When I encountered Candice O'Denver, she was the first person that I knew who truly had stabilised in enlightened consciousness. Through her stability, this enabled me to fast-track exceptionally to my own stabilisation, which in turn has affected thousands and thousands and now millions of beautiful Brothers and Sisters who have been following my work.

It is essential to let everyone know at this stage of this book that when I stabilised in fifth dimensional consciousness, I experienced an almighty Kundalini awakening and homecoming to God-consciousness. This activated a deep state of Samadhi, which included six months of experiencing ecstatic Kundalini rushes consistently.

For that entire time I was bathed in angelic codes, and the remembrance of the truth regarding the divine nature of reality and the eternal abiding divinity of every single one of God's creations.

Enlightenment is Not for the Lazy

So, to conclude this chapter: in my humble opinion, it can never be emphasised enough that enlightenment is not for the faint-hearted and it is definitely not for the lazy.

You have to commit to being empty, to dropping your story every minute of every day. Because every minute of every day, your ego is pulling you into those old patterns and narratives of victimhood and 'poor me.' *Why did this happen to me?* etc. And the reason for this is because this is the very job of the ego.

To be a spiritual master, you have to be on watch 24 hours a day. You have to take full responsibility for the words that you speak and be extremely vigilant at all times about every single thing that you say.

CHAPTER FIVE - COMING HOME TO THE HEART

I would like to take this sacred opportunity to remind us all that one of the most powerful ways that we come home to ourselves in stabilised and abiding spiritual awakeness is by listening to our heart and trusting the messages our heart gives us.

The heart is captain of the ship of your soul, and the vast majority of humanity has woefully forgotten this. Society has indoctrinated everyone to believe that the mind is the master, but nothing could be further from the truth.

I have learned on my spiritual journey that my higher self communicates to me very quietly, almost silently through my heart's subtle vibrations, and whenever I listen to my heart and act upon its guidance, I experience the most extraordinary expansion of my consciousness.

One of the longest-forgotten secrets is that the heart is the GPS that Mother-Father God has placed safely inside us, which is fully equipped to take us to our greatest destiny in the quickest, most efficient route possible.

The heart consciousness has access to our higher self and our subconscious mind which knows about the shortcuts and the pitfalls that lie ahead of us on our journey.

When we listen to and attune to our heart's guidance, this is when we become one with our soul's greatest destiny.

One of the most significant tests or lessons that we have on the spiritual path is remembering that it is safe to believe the heart's beautiful and exquisite voice.

Until I had this epiphany I was believing and following the false guidance of my ego, then one day I woke up and finally realised that my heart's wisdom is who I truly am.

I saw that the messages from my heart are never random. Indeed, my heart contains blueprints that have been strategically placed there to assist specifically in the manifestation of heaven on Earth.

The third-dimensional reality will never reflect this truth back to us. We each have to claim that remembrance just as I had to claim it. And I was waiting; like everyone else, I was waiting for some external figure to grant me permission to listen to, follow and ultimately believe my heart's wisdom and knowing.

May we always remember that paradise is a place within the self, where our soul truly originates. Paradise is the vibration of who we truly are and we must remember that as God's children.

May we all become conscious of the filters that society has imposed upon us, that have been invested in disguising the truth of who we truly are: That we are all sacred and divine Daughters and Sons of Mother-Father God and it is our duty and personal responsibility to awaken to the false programming that the third-dimensional matrix has imposed upon all our creators' most beloved children.

The truth of creation is held within all of our hearts. The third-dimensional illusion has sought to cast a shadow of doubt over the heart consciousness, but may it be remembered forever, that the heart reigns supreme in the living reality of God.

Your heart is the most phenomenal navigational GPS satellite system in the universe, that will take you very, very quickly to your spiritual destiny. However, if you allow your mind to doubt and question your heart, you will hold up your destiny. And it would be wise to note that is a choice that you are making out of fear.

Your heart knows exactly how to lead you to happiness, ecstasy and bliss. Your heart holds the living, undistorted memory of your eternal divine sacred beloved.

It is only the mind that casts doubt over the heart's knowing. If one believes the mind over the heart, then it is important to know that that is a choice that you are making.

Do you believe the powerful voice of your heart? The powerful knowing of your heart? Or do you indulge the voice of your ego? The ego that seeks perpetually to diminish and belittle this sacred GPS's guidance which is doing its utmost to guide you home to happiness, eternal bliss and marriage with your one true love.

You would do well to heed the message of your heart and take actions upon its instruction immediately. As Joseph Campbell says, "Follow your bliss, you will find doors opening for you that previously were closed."

Truly your heart is where you will find your bliss, And it is the heart consciousness that safely stores the living, undistorted memory of your eternal, divine sacred beloved.

Doubt Over the Heart's Knowing

It is only the mind that casts doubt over knowing. And that is a choice that every soul every moment in this free will universe.

As I have mentioned and will mention many, many times, this sacred offering is coming forth from the Zero-point field, where there is no beginning and no end. Where all timelines meet and converge. And so, you will find that I talk about the beginning and I talk about the end, and the middle simultaneously and non-linearly.

We are entering the spiral of creation, the Zero-point field, where all truth co-exists simultaneously, and all timelines run concurrently.

Now would be a perfect moment to rest your mind for a short moment.

Telepathy from the Heart

Telepathy has been widely misunderstood within the third-dimensional realm. Telepathy is how hearts communicate with each other. Telepathy is how spirits communicate with each other.

We must remember that our third-dimensional physical form is temporary in nature. However, our spirits, our souls are eternal.

When we drop into the heart space and communicate telepathically with those we love, we tap into a communication strand that has existed within eternity forever.

In the vast majority of cases, I have been shown that the divine feminine takes on the mantle of agreeing to awaken first, to connect with her divine counterpart on the higher dimensional realms, so that he can receive messages of comfort, support and belonging. Reminding him that he did not incarnate into this world alone, that he incarnated to be in perpetual union with his best friend, throughout all of eternity.

The third-dimensional realm would have you believe that telepathy is very mystical and somewhat even questionable, but nothing could be further from the truth. The heart is the most powerful organ in the body and has an enormous electromagnetic field. Whenever we think about somebody and connect with them from the heart space, this bypasses all time and space; the codes and frequencies instantly reach them. This is because all hearts are connected to the infinity of all that is.

It is almost impossible to receive a telepathic message if your vessel is filled up with illusory third-dimensional programming. However, if you have done the necessary work to release yourself of the false programming and have become an empty vessel again, you are much more likely to receive telepathic messages as and when they are sent to you.

People often ask me how to send a telepathic message, and I always say to them, "You have to have the consciousness of a child when you send a telepathic message. Simply connect to your heart space, think of the person you wish to contact and then start speaking very innocently from your heart."

I have found that very often you will hear an automatic response from the person you are contacting; but generally, what the mind does is reject that response and convince us that we are making things up and imagining a reply.

Every time we choose to deny the message that we have just received, in effect, we are shutting down our telepathic channel.

The trick is to believe the response you hear.

For example, if you contact your Twin Flame telepathically and say, “Hi beloved, I miss you so much. I’m thinking about you today, do you have a message for me?” And then deep within you, you hear your Twin say, “I miss you too, and I’m thinking about you today.” What usually happens at this stage is that the person receiving the message entirely rejects what they have clearly heard and assumes that they are making it up and being childish. If we have this attitude this completely and entirely shuts down our telepathic channel.

We all need to go with the initial message that is being sent to us and keep nodding our head, saying “Yes.” If we do this, the messages will become extremely powerful, deep, complex and very often in my experience, very emotional.

Intense crying and laughter is very often a hallmark of having true and genuine telepathic communication with someone that you love.

Contact Your Twin Flame Blessing

So, let’s try it. Please take a moment now to drop into your heart space and send a telepathic message to your divine consort, your Twin Flame, who most likely is suffering from PTSD from being born into the matrix and being separated from you.

Many divine masculine polarity Twin Flames have completely and utterly forgotten the memo that indeed they are Twin Flames and have decided to move forward with life on Earth from very much a survival vibration.

Please know that your Twin Flame is waiting for you to be in contact with him or her on the higher planes of consciousness and it is highly advised that you activate this telepathic connection as soon as possible.

So, you are invited now to take a moment to drop into your heart and send a telepathic message to your Twin Flame that you are here on Earth, that you are both resting under the same moon, under the same sun, that you can both see the same stars in the sky. Please tell them that you are doing everything to prepare for this powerful and sacred union and you are working on becoming the highest, most masterful version of yourself.

After you have sent the message, listen very deeply and take note of the message you receive back. At this stage, most people deny the message and decide that their imagination is making things up. The trick, though, to becoming a master telepathic communicator is to believe the message that your heart is telling you. So, go ahead and say thank you for responding to me and now begin a conversation very innocently, as a child.

I highly recommend that you connect telepathically with your Twin Flame at least once a day - to alleviate any depression that they may be experiencing on a soul level from not having any contact with you and from (in many cases) forgetting the soul memo that you would reunite in this lifetime.

The heart is the most powerful organ in the body and it has a vast and substantial electromagnetic field. You are eternally connected to your Twin Flame via your heart consciousness. Every time you permit yourself to drop into your heart, to send out an innocent, childlike message from your heart to your Twin Flame, he or she will receive that message. This message will help them so profoundly and so deeply to find the courage and the sustenance to get through life on Earth whilst preparing to reunite with you on the physical level.

As we go further into this book, there will be so many codes, so many downloads and so many activations that will be made available to you. These will help you quickly come into sacred and eternal physical union with your highest divine consort.

AND SO, IT IS.

Please know that I have brought through a very powerful chapter in the accompanying workbook that goes along with this book that teaches you and guides you how to have very high-level telepathic contact with your divine counterpart.

Every Moment the Universe Hands us a Blank Canvas

It can never ever be stressed enough that the heart centre is the key to your awakening.

In the third dimensional matrix, we are heavily indoctrinated to believe that we are victims; but the truth is, we are all creator beings.

In every single moment, Mother-Father God hands us a blank canvas for us to create precisely whatever our heart desires, as we are all creator beings.

When the false idea of guilt and shame is fully cleared, and when we have done the alchemical work of parenting our own wounded, abandoned child self, it is then, and only then, that we unfreeze the frozen areas of our heart, to allow the flow of divine love to pour forth unceasingly.

It is my greatest wish at this point in time that all of you who are reading these words take a moment to acknowledge how far we have all come. Back home to God, back home to sacred union, back home to this profound conversation that we are having.

Now would be a perfect time to rest your mind for a short moment.

CHAPTER SIX - 144,000

Who are the 144,000 Lightworkers?

Who are the 144,000 lightworkers that are referenced at the beginning of this book? The 144,000 are represented in all spiritual prophecies, from the Book of Enoch and many other books in the Bible. The 144,000 refers to the return of the Bird Tribe.

There are many great mysteries spoken about the 144,000 and many reference the return of the Bird Tribe in the turning of the great wheel in this great transition from a third-dimensional hell realm to fifth-dimensional heaven.

The Bird Tribe are those of us who have for the vast majority of our lifetimes on the earthly plane resided in indigenous bodies, at one with the Earth, in tune with the cycles and the rhythms of nature. Every step that we walk is a prayer to Mother Earth. Every word that we speak is a blessing of gratitude to her.

The Bird Tribe are embodiments of the higher codes of unconditional love and self-mastery. We are here to hold humanity's hand as we all step up as graciously as possible into the higher dimensional realms of consciousness. The Bird Tribe are also connected to the founder race of Lyra, who are also known as the feline beings.

I would like to explain further that which I have been shown regarding the significance of the 144 code and how it pertains to Twin soul union.

My understanding of the 144,000 is connected to the big bang. My spirit team showed me that before the moment of the big bang, all that existed was one large ovoid sphere of light. It was then decreed, at some point within the life journey of this ovoid sphere of light, that it would split in order to know itself, see itself, taste itself, dance with itself, hear itself and ultimately reunite with itself.

As I mentioned at the beginning of the book, at the time of this original split, 144,000 identical fractals of the original source template split off from creation, and they formed the first monadic soul group or soul structure.

This group is the original founder group of creation and went forth to birth planetary star systems such as Lyra and many other planetary systems.

The 144,000 was the first original monadic soul group that split from source energy. And within the 144,000 souls evolutionary sojourn it was at some point decreed that those original units (comprised of 144,000 units of equalised balanced polarity energy of masculine and feminine energy) would make the monumental decision to split from itself and thus go on its own individualised journey, ultimately to be reunited again for the upliftment and benefit of the universal matrix.

The 144,000 code is very much connected to a call that went out - a mythic call, heralding this great shift of Ages from the Age of Pisces to the Age of Aquarius.

Right now, in human evolution, it would be an extremely obvious time for the 144,000 Bird Tribe to return to the earthly plane in their Twin Flame pairs; in order to be the teachers, leaders, facilitators, guides and way-showers they have always been throughout all dimensional realms of consciousness.

The Earth matrix has proven to be extremely challenging, even for the original founder monadic soul group: the original 144,000. It has been a long and arduous journey for even some of those members of that group to truly awaken out of the grips of the matrix; particularly the divine masculines.

However, this is very much shifting now as so many divine masculines are waking up in this current energetic climate.

The 144,000 is also a master number. One plus four plus four, equals nine and nine is the number of completion. Numerologically, there is nowhere to go within its singular trajectory when we reach number nine. This represents the ending and it represents completion.

What comes after nine is ten, a one and a zero. Zero represents the Zero-point field of consciousness. One represents the first and tenth digit in the cycle of our numerological system. It is important to note, that every time we add a zero on to any number, it exponentially increases in value, and any mysteries can be revealed in this one simple observation.

The 144 code is a master number and a signal code for our DNA, which informs our dormant sleeping DNA that it's time to come out of its asleep, comatose phase, into the vibratory frequency of activation and awakeness. Therefore, the 144 code is intricately connected to trigger points within our own DNA memory release system.

As we are now in the time of the great awakening, the number code 144,000 is hugely important and symbolic. It is symbolic of our collective monadic oversoul that has come forth to fully assist in the great shift from the third dimension to the fifth dimension.

Numbers as Ascension Trigger Codes

That is why many Starseeds often see the number 144, just as we often see the numbers 11:11. These numbers are Ascension trigger codes that we have agreed to work with, prior to our incarnation. These codes are connected to the activation of dormant strands within our DNA which were tampered with at the fall of Atlantis.

It was decreed at the time of Atlantis that humanity's DNA would be allowed to be tampered with. This third-dimensional agenda sought to create a confusion in the perfect patterning of God's creation through the scrambling of our 12-strand diamond formation DNA patterning.

Because of this, it was deemed necessary from the higher dimensional realms that particular codes and triggers would be sent to us at specific times in order to awaken us out of this lower frequency programming matrix that has induced spiritual amnesia upon all of God's precious children.

This triggering activation occurs when we see repeating numbers such as 11:11 and powerful master numbers such as 144.

When we come forth as souls with a mission to fully awaken in this lifetime, in the eternal moment of now, we agree to work with specific number patterns in a synchronistic manner. This means that an agreement is made between source and each individualised soul aspect that these number sequences would flash to us in the third-dimensional matrix, indicating that our personal awakening trajectory is upon us.

This serves to remind us that what we have been programmed to believe is by no means the be-all and end-all.

In fact, it is a lie of the highest order and these number codes appearing prolifically with great synchronicity and tenacity are connected to agreements that we made in our pre-birth state; whereby the universe would send forth these codes to assist in our inevitable awakening.

Fourth Dimensional Consciousness

Once the door of the third dimension has been opened, this opens us up to fourth-dimensional consciousness. This is a realm filled with Fairies, Dragons, Reptiles and Archons - filled with all manner of beings of extreme light polarity and extreme dark polarity. There are currently many souls on the Earth plane that are stuck in fourth-dimensional consciousness and this can invoke feelings of empowerment, yet without the clarity of being fully stabilized in Unity consciousness.

It is not until we reach fifth-dimensional consciousness, which is the Zero-point - the place where all duality merges - that there is an awakening and knowing to the truth, that one is in eternal and perpetual union with Mother-Father God and all that is.

The Zero-Point Field

As soon as one has experienced the inner alchemical marriage, the Heiros Gamos, this sends forth the codes into the collective that one has truly arrived home in the Zero-point field of consciousness, which is akin to fifth-dimensional consciousness.

As will be repeated over and over in this sacred scripture in order to offer an antidote to the horrific, hateful programming of the third dimension, fifth-dimensional consciousness is the consciousness of sacred union, of sacred marriage, where the word Yoga derives from.

Yoga means union; union with God, union with self, union with nature, union with your masculine and feminine energies within and union with your eternal partner on all planes of consciousness.

In fifth-dimensional consciousness, one remembers - I am a divine eternal avatar being and my consciousness is not fixed to the third dimension. My consciousness is attuned to all higher dimensional realms and this is because I have learnt to place the voice of my heart, the guidance of my sacred heart, the knowing of my heart, as the master: the captain of my ship. I have surrendered to that silent, still, powerful knowing of the heart that is forever guiding me home to the eternal moment of now.

One clearly remembers that as I align my consciousness with the Zero-point field and truly come home to fifth-dimensional consciousness. This is the vibration that automatically lifts Gaia out of the third-dimensional prison matrix into the fifth-dimensional New Earth, Golden Age, heaven-on-Earth template, and this is precisely the mission that all of us Starseeds have come forth to accomplish.

We multiple, dimensionally awakened beings have remote viewed and seen that this mission is successful beyond measure. This is because the light has already won on the higher dimensional realms of consciousness and now it is merely a holographic catch-up game being played out on the 3D dimension.

Humanity is being asked to very carefully choose which timelines they are existing and co-creating on.

Are you still choosing to exist on the third-dimensional fear-porn timeline? Or are you choosing not to?

Have you turned off all mainstream media? One would hope so if you are reading this book.

"Have you realised that you are not and never have been a victim?"

You Are A Creator Being

This one sentence sums up the entire crux of being spiritually awakened.

The 12-Strand DNA

For those who are asleep in the third-dimensional matrix, there is a deep false program running that perpetually says that *I am a victim.* This programming was allowed to be implemented into humanity's consciousness at the time of the fall of Atlantis, when permission from on high was granted enabling humanity's DNA to be taken out of its 12- strand diamond perfection formation and placed into a two-strand formation, thus scrambling the remaining ten strands and naming them junk DNA.

The 12-strand DNA is the gateway to multiple dimensional, ALL-strand DNA activation and alignment, just as the fifth-dimensional consciousness is the gateway to full, multiple dimensional levels of consciousness.

When this scrambling occurred, this caused great confusion in the sacred DNA map that Mother-Father God gave his and her children that would help them come home to the remembrance of their divinity.

No one is ever a victim; all is perfect. Our souls agreed to have this experience at the time of Atlantis, so that we could experience The Awakening and sacred Union that is going on now in this time of The Great Awakening on planet Earth.

As I write these words, it is the 16th December 2020 and we are five days away from Jupiter and Saturn's grand conjunction who are indeed 1.11 degree apart in this moment of this time of writing.

The Fall of Atlantis

At the time of Atlantis, this sacred map home to abiding perpetual remembrance of our divinity was tampered with and this created significant confusion for God's children. Indeed, this is what we are all awakening from and recorrecting right now in this time of Mother Earth's Great Ascension.

This book is a perpetual celebration of remembrance of one child of God's experience. It will serve you well to remember that this is my own direct experience that I am sharing. Nothing here is purported as eternal truth. This is an invitation always to the reader to practice discernment. If something resonates for you it's true, if it doesn't resonate for you it's not true for you. Please respect your body wisdom and your sacred intuition.

It is my most profound honour to serve all of my Brothers and Sisters at all times because the nectar that I drank on top of the Himalayan mountains when I was 21 truly was an overdose of God-consciousness. The second I had the experience my heart wanted to give it all away to all my Brothers and Sisters, so that everyone would remember the truth that exists beyond the lie of what has been told to us.

We are sacred, precious beings, beloved children of the most high. The holiest force in all of existence is our creator and we are all offspring of that. Isn't it incredible that no one ever told us that!?

God is not an old man in the sky with a long beard judging anyone. That is the greatest lie ever told. God is love - God is eternal love - the beginning and the end and God is everything in between.

God is the Alpha and Omega; God is your Brother and Sister, your Father, your Uncle and your child. God is all that is: every grain of sand, every blade of grass and every star in the sky.

There is nothing in creation that is not God. God is so great and is continuously birthing extraordinarily ecstatic, clear, beautiful creations in every moment.

God is everywhere and in everything and this book is a promise from your higher self that you will fully, fully remember that you are an eternal divine child of God. You promised your lineage that you would be the one to step forward as the spiritual leader, no longer looking for approval from any of the asleep Brothers and Sisters surrounding you who have been attached to staying locked in third-dimensional consciousness, also known as caterpillar consciousness.

This book holds the precise codes that will activate your DNA from the time of Atlantis and Lemuria.

This is an invitation for you to fully and completely remember your divinity, your innocence and the fact that you are so deeply loved by Mother-Father God.

Imagine a mother and her newborn child and times that by a million every second - that is how much God loves you and how much God loves all of us.

Mother-Father God has zero favourites - that is one of the greatest illusions of all - Mother-Father God loves all his/her children equally and every one of us is special to God.

These words on these pages are the map that we also created at the time of Lemuria that would work specifically with the 144,000 Starseeds who have incarnated to become the spiritual lighthouses, the spiritual leaders, of the birthing of the great new Golden Age.

It is time now, children of the rainbow, children of the sun, to take your mantle and wear your crown with pride. You are of the Royal lineage of God's creation; you hold the Royal bloodline. You promised your Brothers and Sisters that you would wear your crown with pride, in full remembrance of your sacred divinity and innocence as a child of the eternal creator of all that is.

These words are filled with codes that will activate dormant DNA strands to start making patterns and sparks towards each other, creating synapses and fusing links - creating the map back to your complete remembrance of your divinity - your perpetual innocence as Mothers / Fathers / Daughters / Sons / Granddaughters and Grandsons.

Please remember as you are reading these words that this is a very life-transforming experience for all of us and it would be a profound act of generosity if we could all pass on this sacred book to those whom we deeply love.

Passing on this message to someone that we truly love is how this book will reach the hearts and consciousness of all of our Brothers and Sisters. This book is destined to set the whole world alight with spiritual truth.

It would serve us all well to remember that whenever we share this book, we are truly offering those who we love the opportunity for their 12-strand DNA patterning to be thoroughly reformed, that they may have access to this sacred map which will guide them home to the remembrance of their divinity.

Dearest ones, in your hands you hold a scripture that is a specific map with many, many keys. If you listen deeply with your heart, as you are reading these words, know that you are truly entering into the Kingdom of heaven, the Queendom of heaven. The place of sacred union that exists within you, that exists within your heart, as your heart is the place of sacred union, the place where heaven and Earth meet.

There is so much to be spoken about the 144,000 and indeed about the 144 code. Indeed, many encyclopedias of information are stored within the Akashic records about this precise subject. I pray that these words trigger your own downloads and your own sacred memories of whether you are part of that original group that split from source energy.

Signs of an Old Soul

Have you always considered yourself to be an old soul? Do children and animals love you very dearly and are very drawn to your energy? Do people often cry in your presence? And do people reveal their deepest held secrets to you often? Do you consider yourself to be a planetary elder? And are you in absolute full remembrance that you are an innocent child of God? These are all hallmarks and qualities of one who truly is part of the 144,000, and is truly an old soul.

This is not a hierarchical system being spoken about here. This is how creation was created. And the truth is that every single one of God's children holds the 144,000 master code patterning within them because the 144,000 code represents full remembrance of your eternal and inherent divinity and innocence as a child of God.

No matter how old your soul is or how young your soul is, the moment one person aligns with the truth that they are an innocent child of God they automatically become part of the 144,000, and activate the 144,000 master code within them.

Therefore, it is also a metaphorical and symbolic number because spirit is non-linear and non-black and white, which are very much the hallmarks of perception within the third dimension.

When the 144,000 code is spoken about, it is crucial to perceive it in a non-linear way and understand that this is a multi-dimensional code that is intrinsically connected to the awakening of humanity.

I believe that as we are now in the time of the Great Awakening, the number 144,000 is symbolic of our collective, monadic oversoul which has come forth to fully assist in the great shift from the third dimension to the fifth dimension.

CHAPTER SEVEN - ATLANTIS

Atlantis and Lemuria

In a story that is cyclical and non-linear, with no beginning and truly no end, it is always interesting the places where we choose to start as an entry point into this vast exploration of creational reality. I am being nudged by my higher self-team to devote the next chapter of this book to share with you all what I've been shown with regards to what took place at the time of the creation of Lemuria and Atlantis.

As I've said, everything that I share has never been regurgitated from anybody else's research. Everything I share is based on direct downloads, visions, synchronicities, dreams, inner knowing and communication from my higher self.

I am shown timelines and this is what I am sharing with you all in this book. I'm inviting you, the reader, to practice discernment of the highest order. And if these words resonate for you, then they are a message to you from your higher self. If these messages do not ring true for you, then this message is not for you and that is perfectly in alignment with the perfection of creation.

Now would be a great time to rest as awareness for a moment.

I would like to now go into a deep sharing about what has been revealed to me about what took place with regards to the creation of humanity.

I was shown that the Earth has been through many deep cleanses and cataclysms in her trillions and trillions of years of existence. And at a point, probably within 500,000 to 1,000,000 years ago, after a very, very significant cataclysmic cleanse, I was shown that there were many Pleiadian ships flying around Earth's atmosphere. The beings that resided in the ships were able to observe the somewhat fledgling Earth planet, endowed with beautiful flowers, plants and water and with a great temperature.

Pleiadian Light Ships

As these ships were hovering around Earth's atmosphere, I was shown that they decided with the permission of Mother-Father God that they would colonise the earthly plane. And I was shown that as these Pleiadian ships entered into Earth's atmosphere, they bought with them many beings and technologies from high-dimensional realms of consciousness.

These ships were extremely vast in nature and they contained up to one million beings, including animals and plants. I was shown that these Pleiadian ships landed on the earthly plane many, many eons ago and they created with their highly advanced technology the crystalline cities of Lemuria.

My spirit team has shown me that Pleiadian beings are sixth-dimensional beings and above. So, when they entered down into the earthly plane, they did not have carbon thir-

dimensional forms as we do today. They co-existed in their higher dimensional crystalline light forms.

At the time of Lemuria, there existed a great and fantastical angelic race which was consumed by vibrations of ecstasy and bliss. Spirit revealed to me that at the time of Lemuria many of the 144,000 Twin soul pairs were incarnated.

These were part of the 144,000 original monadic structure which separated in a fractal manner at the beginning of creation.

More on Lemuria

At the time of Lemuria, it was soul contracted or seeded, you could say, that these Twin Flames would come back together in eternal and perpetual union, after the Earth itself went through an incredible exploration of polarity from light to dark then back to light again.

The beings of Lemuria were able to read the passages of time and they were able to see precisely what would happen, through observing the astrological movements of the stars.

At the time of Lemuria, there was an expansion of sorts that took place whereby Lemuria did not experience a cataclysmic descent. Instead, spirit showed me that it actually merged with that, which became known as Atlantis. It is my understanding that as that which is known as Atlantis anchored onto the earthly realm, there was a shift from a sixth-dimensional Lemurian crystalline form/society to a more fifth-dimensional crystalline form/society.

Therefore, it would seem right to assume that Atlantis grew out of the culture of Lemuria and then somehow became its own vibrational reality.

Atlantis

Until the fall of Atlantis, the Earth's electromagnetic field was protected by on high from any external attacks. But during a particular period at the time of Atlantis, it was decreed by Mother-Father God and the highest forces of creation that a vulnerability would be allowed to be placed within the electromagnetic seal of the Earth, thus enabling, for the first time, nefarious energies to enter into the Earth's atmosphere.

As this seal was broken, this vulnerability activated an influx of lower-dimensional energy from the star system of Mars (which is also connected to the lower-dimensional fractals of the planet Nibiru).

As this nefarious energy entered into the Earth's atmosphere, it bought the consciousness of control and separation for the first time. Resulting in the beautiful, sweet children of God, these Twin Flame pairs, whose divine sacred unions were seeded at the time of Lemuria, to experience a cataclysmic separation from each other.

Many of you who are reading these words will be feeling extremely deep emotions right now, as the trauma of the split that occurred at the time of Atlantis is stored deeply within our memory and cells, awaiting the divine moment to be triggered and released.

Please know, Brothers and Sisters, that the trauma that took place at the time of Atlantis must be brought out of the shadows. We must address this collective wound that occurred particularly for the 144,000 Starseeds at the time of the fall of Atlantis.

Up until this cataclysmic shift in energies, the Twins were very powerful and very solid in their union. And it must be noted that because of this, because of the sacredness of the true Twin Flames and the energies that they were holding and anchoring for the collective, this is precisely what kept Earth's atmospheric grid fully stabilised in its crystalline, fifth-dimensional vibratory frequency band.

As this nefarious, lower fourth-dimensional energy was allowed to enter into Earth's grid, as mentioned before, it brought with it the consciousness of control and separation. And it was indeed these Twin Flame unions that were specifically targeted by these nefarious energies. Then, for the first time, many divine masculines were lured away to go and fight in wars over land and ownership.

Separation was a concept that was not considered a possibility at the time of Lemuria and early Atlantis. This was an imposter vibration that was allowed to enter externally, thus bringing the Earth's consciousness into a lower vibratory field.

Many people know that Atlantis's fall is also very much connected to many high Atlantean souls being targeted explicitly when these nefarious energies were permitted to enter into Earth's atmosphere.

These nefarious beings manipulated many of these high-level beings to use the powers they had access to, to serve themselves and their dimensional Warlords, as opposed to serving the collective.

As soon as these nefarious energies took over, this activated the vibrational drop of Atlantis, which is now referred to as the fall of Atlantis. This refers explicitly to Atlantis falling out of the fifth-dimensional realm, into the lower fourth dimension and now ultimately into the third dimension and now going back up to the fifth dimension again. As this occurred, the Twin Flame pairs were specifically targeted and many, many of the divine masculine Twin Flames were lured off to go and serve in these lower-dimensional conflicts over land and ownership. This is why many of the divine masculines to this day still hold very deep scars and wounds with regards to feeling an incredible amount of guilt, due to them leaving and abandoning their true divine Twin Flame.

I was shown that the divine masculines' core wound is a feeling of deep guilt for abandoning their divine feminine, and it has become absolutely apparent that for many of the original 144,000 divine feminines, many of their core wounds are abandonment; the deep fear of being abandoned.

Many of the 144,000 Twin Flame collective experienced this core wound that occurred at the time of Atlantis, when we experienced a cataclysmic separation from our divine counterpart, which caused an exceptional and profound tear in the fabric of our soul's etheric patterning.

The trauma that we all experienced at the time of Atlantis has been stored so deeply in our cells, awaiting the time of now, the time of the great planetary awakening, to be fully addressed and healed.

We are now bearing witness to this great astrological alignment of planets in Aquarius, at this monumental time in our planet's evolutionary journey. This is bringing back deep memories of the wise elders of Atlantis and Lemuria, who knew that these sacred unions, that were seeded at the time of Lemuria, would bear fruit and once again manifest triumphantly on the physical plane at this time of now, the great shift.

More on Atlantis

It is so important that memories of Atlantis are brought out of the unconscious because it reminds us that we are truly multi-dimensional avatar beings and we are blessed with the innate ability to time travel back to the time of any period, including Atlantis and Lemuria. We are able do this in order to rescript and restore those timelines whereby extremely deep, traumatic incidents took place.

In fact, we can shift the script entirely, whereby there is no separation whatsoever. This is highly recommended for all souls that are truly on the Twin soul path and I pray that this sharing will inspire you to pursue this deep work to heal that trauma that you are carrying with regards to what occurred at the time of Atlantis.

Please see the chapter in my upcoming workbook about Atlantis. I highly recommend the exercises and meditations that go along with the workbook. They will help you very deeply to heal and restore this deep core wound.

In Closing This Chapter

The purpose of this chapter has been to activate soul memories of your fifth-dimensional consciousness experience, as a being at the time of Lemuria and Atlantis, so that you may connect energetically with the 12-strand diamond structure DNA patterning, prior to its tampering which occurred when these nefarious energies were allowed to enter into the earthly plane.

The purpose of this chapter is to give you a context as to why so many of your relationships have collapsed due to unprocessed trauma that exists at a deep unconscious level of your personal being and within the being of the collective.

The purpose of this chapter is to remind you that you are an avatar being and you have a duty and responsibility to change timelines and adapt scripts in order to restore traumatic experiences of separation that have taken place within your soul's evolutionary journey. This is all part of the levelling up that we do, as we align with our true codes of spiritual mastery.

You are not a victim of any of your circumstances, regardless of what you have experienced in the past. All of those experiences have contributed to your own personal soul's expansion and to the expansion of the entire universe. You chose every single one of your experiences, including the separation from your Twin Flame at the time of Atlantis. Therefore, you have the power to go forth and transform that script, to rewrite that timeline, so that you can implement into your etheric memory bank a brand new timeline whereby the split or separation that occurred at the time does not actually occur.

This is how powerful you are; this is how powerful we are. This is what has been hidden from us for eons: the fact that we are multiple-dimensional avatar beings who have a duty and responsibility to work with all timelines that our soul has experienced, in order to correct and recalibrate them to their highest unity timeline potential.

It is my deep and sincere hope that this chapter has restored memories and has been a significant dot connector for you.

Now would be a great time to rest your mind for a short moment.

CHAPTER EIGHT - THE PASSAGE OF TIME

The passage of time has been recorded by all planetary elders since the moment this Earth was seeded with creation. Through the astrological transits, the great planetary elders could see the precise movements and passages within history and her-story. Thus, all that occurred at the time of Lemuria and Atlantis and indeed to this very moment, has been foreseen by all of our planetary elders.

All long count calendars end at the time period between 2012 and 2020. The Mayan, the Inca, the Sanskrit calendars and the Egyptian calendars, indeed all of the long count lunar calendars, end at this particular epoch in time.

May we all remember that there is a reason that those watching the transition of the stars in the night sky knew about occurrences that would be taking place throughout this planet's evolutionary destiny. It was noted by all of these planetary elders who originated from star systems such as Sirius and the Pleiades that this great shift, this great transformation, would be culminating at this great time of now in 2020, just as we enter into December 21st and beyond: The 2020 Ascension event portal.

These long-term calendars ended at this particular epoch in time and the reason for this is that this time period represents the end of time as we know it; the end of third-dimension linear time.

The Earth is truly on her Ascension towards fifth-dimensional consciousness. This is the entry point into the Zero-point field of consciousness that represents time and no time simultaneously. This is what was referred to with regards to the ending of these long count calendars.

At the time of Atlantis, it was agreed that the Twin soul units would have an experience of separation so that their soul could literally separate into its own individualised form. This would mean that each soul would get to experience duality and polarity in order to ultimately come back together with itself, with God and with its divine other. This would ensure the experience of rapturous bliss and ecstasy and ultimately the Ascension of one's consciousness. This happens every time a Twin Flame pair separates and is reunited again.

This is the eternal dance of the Twin souls.

We are one in the heart of God's truth and we agreed to separate in order to come back together. Every time that we separate and come back together, we bring vaster and more expansive experiences to our unit.

What is a Timeline?

A timeline is created based upon attention and intention; whatever it is that you believe will create a timeline, which is essentially a holographic reality in and of itself. There are an infinite number of timelines operating concurrently within the present moment of now and wherever it is that we choose to focus our attention and intention is the timeline that we will empower and create in any given moment. It is important to note that in any given moment, we are working with personal timelines and we are working with collective timelines.

The programming of the third dimension would have you believe that a timeline is permanently fixed but a timeline is in fact fluid. Once you are truly awakened, you realise that you have a responsibility to address any timelines in your energetic field that are stuck. You quickly remember that a timeline stays stuck if a trauma occurs and you do not manage to heal and alchemise it.

If you do not address the place where there is frozen energy, if you just allow that frozen energy to remain unaddressed within your energetic field, you are essentially inhibiting yourself from a certain flow of Pranic life force energy that is perpetually streaming forth from your higher self but is unable to move freely in your energetic field.

This is why it is so important to work with timelines, so that we can clear blocked energy.

Also, in our fully awakened state it becomes glaringly apparent that we are being guided by our higher self, soul consciousness, to work with future timelines. When we work with the sacred union of our divine soul, we remember that we are eternally in sacred union with our divine consort on the fifth-dimensional plane of consciousness and from that higher perspective there has never, ever been any separation between us.

When we truly arrive home in the Zero-point field of consciousness, into the deep oceanic waters of eternal union with our divine eternal consort, within and without, we enter into a vibration of perpetual satiety, where there is zero lack and we experience the eternal dance of our sacred union with our beloved Twin Flame on all multi-dimensional levels of consciousness, fifth and above.

The fifth dimension is the gateway to remembrance of our full multiple-dimensional consciousness and is the gateway point whereby we access the sixth, seventh, eighth dimensions and above.

The fifth dimension is the opening gateway. Once our consciousness has arrived home and stabilized in the fifth dimension, our spiritual journey by no means ends there. There is a continuous expansion into higher dimensional realms of consciousness and the experience of the individual being able to hold the vibration of God, with a greater and greater depth and capacity.

One of the most striking side effects affecting those who have truly awakened and come home to fifth-dimensional consciousness are they are very aware and very proactive in the knowing of their Twin soul, who they are, and what is occurring for them.

This is all part of the powerful, sacred gifts that being truly, truly awakened brings forth. The knowing that there's never a need, per se, to be with your Twin Flame on the physical level, as you are always perpetually conjoined on the higher planes of consciousness.

If you are experiencing a need or a lack in yourself or an overwhelming desire to be with your Twin Flame, then this is not the time for you to be with your Twin Flame.

You are the cake. You are the icing. You are the cherry on top. Your Twin Flame is the hundred and thousands that God comes and sprinkles right at the very end.

It is your divine self that you are actually looking for.

Until you realise who you are you will never be a true vibrational match for your eternal divine consort.

Everyone has been put under a spell that says that when they are united with their Twin Flame, their search will be over and life will be perfect. However, I feel that I have a duty and responsibility to share with you my own direct experience, that this is simply not true.

I have discovered that what the soul is truly seeking is the present moment, and the abiding knowing that it is at one with God, one with the universe…

Your soul in its infinite wisdom is astute in the knowing that it is only when it finds its true self and the abiding peace and knowing that comes from that, will it stand a chance of uniting with its divine eternal vibrational consort on all planes of consciousness.

The satiety that comes from experiencing zero lack in one's consciousness is precisely the energy which calls forth and magnetises the Twin Flame, not the energy of seeking, searching, needing and desperate longing.

Of course, on the Twin soul path there is a longing, but this is the longing of the soul and this is very beautiful. We each have that place inside of us where there is a sweet and sacred longing for our divine counterpart, if we are in physical separation from our Twin Flame.

This, though, is not an opportunity to indulge in a victim narrative or vibration. This is a sweet longing and a knowing that whatever it is that we intend and wherever it is that we place our attention on as God beings, is precisely what we are manifesting into our physical reality.

A Further Explanation of Twin Flames.

At this conjecture of the birthing of this sacred scripture, it is important for me to share with you all that I am being directed by spirit to repeat important teachings throughout this book.

Subject matters will be shared and woven into the story in unique ways, with the sole purpose of being an antithesis to the false matrix programming that we have all been subjected to.

Therefore, you will hear me speak about subject matters more than once but please know there is a very important reason for this.

Bearing that in mind, I would like to now speak in further depth about what I've been shown about the original Twin Souls and their split from source energy.

I was shown that as the 144 souls holding the identical fractal patterning of the 144 godhead, descended from the ovoid light, it was decreed that the original split would comprise of an androgynous unit and that this androgynous unit would stay in its blissful unified state as an androgynous pair for quite some time, holding and containing both the masculine and feminine polarity energies within it.

I was shown that we traversed the universe for billions and trillions of years as these androgynous beings; having wonderful experiences of expansion, whilst forever in perfect unison with the source of all that is.

At some point in our evolutionary sojourn it was decreed from the highest creator in existence that we, in our androgynous state, would make a somewhat treacherous yet deeply spiritually ordained split from each other, our original source mate.

We would become one individualised masculine polarity and one individualised feminine polarity, so that we may go forth into creational existence to experience expansion and a further deepening into the understanding of who we truly are.

These experiences would ultimately be brought back to our unified Merkarbic field, thus contributing enormously to the overall expansion of the Multiverse.

At this point it is important to remember that our identical Merkabah stays intact forever and remains untainted by any of our experiences, forever remaining a mirror to our Twin.

It would serve us all to remember that the primary reason it was decreed that we as Twin Flames would separate on our individualised journeys was predominately for the sole purpose of reuniting, and in turn bringing forth into the lower planes, the codes of the highest vibratory bliss known in the universe.

When true Twin souls unite after a painful yet illusory period of separation, all of the vibratory bliss codes that are activated through this monumental homecoming spark off codons in one's DNA, that are directly linked to the moment of creation - the orgasm between Mother-Father God, the moment creation was birthed.

Every time a Twin soul pair unites after eons of apparent separation, this sends out ripples throughout the entire universe and connects the entire collective with the original song of creation, which is directly connected to every living being's heart.

We are all one. We are all children of God. We are all Brothers and Sisters. We are all related. We are all offspring of divinity. We are all offspring of the most high. We are one big, huge family. And when one of us experiences the highest rapture of divinity in physical form, the ripples that are sent out into the entire collective and beyond are so extraordinarily powerful that a blast of eternal and pristine love of the creator is sent out as a pulse, and is felt by every single one of God's children.

Every single one of God's creations experience this pulse and are uplifted by this pulse.

This is why it is so important at this sacred time that if you are on the Starseed path - the awakening path - you do the necessary work to awaken to the abiding and perpetual truth of your inherent innocence, the remembrance that you are a sacred, beloved and eternal child of God, and that you live in a world that will never (at this time) reflect that Eternal truth back to you. You must take ownership of that knowing in every moment and you must do this for all your Brothers and Sisters.

Inner Alchemical Marriage Codes

The quickest and most powerful way for you to come into sacred union with your Twin Flame is to activate the sacred, inner alchemical marriage codes that are within your very own being.

In order to manifest the triumphant and eternal union with your divine counterpart, your best mate in the whole of creation, you have to come to the place within yourself where you are eternally and consistently experiencing the satiety of your own inner union with your divine self.

It is so important that you come to a place of fullness and completion within your own self and to a place where there is no need or necessity for you to have your Twin Flame with you on the physical plane.

When you have reached this vibrational plateau, it is then simply a matter of cosmic seconds before your Twin Flame manifests on the physical outer planes of consciousness, for "as it is within, so it is without."

I hope that these words inspire you to remember the importance of doing the inner work.

Please know that all of the tools that I have shared with you in this book and in the accompanying workbook are designed precisely to bring you to that place of satiety and oneness with your own divine presence.

I hope and pray that these words are activating and triggering deep ancient memories within you about your true souls origin and are serving to connect many of the dots, connecting you back to your own higher self, whereby all this sacred knowledge is stored safely and securely in the Akashic fields.

May these words trigger your heart consciousness to open so much that you begin to receive the high angelic codes and messages that are continually streaming forth from your eternal self as you connect to this high stream of consciousness that is flowing through. May you remember to give eternal thanks to the great benevolent forces in the universe that created multi-dimensional love, in all its myriad forms.

May you remember that you are God in physical human form and you are eternally a beloved Daughter or Son of Mother-Father God and as Mother-Father God's eternal creation; Mother-Father God has created a playground of the greatest ecstatic possibility for you, her divine offspring, to perpetually explore. And of course, that includes dancing in eternal and ecstatic bliss with your best friend, your divine consort, the one who sprang forth from the Great White ovoid light with you at the moment of your soul's creation.

The love that Mother-Father God has stored for us within our destiny truly is a fairy tale of the highest order. It would serve us all well to remember that God is truth and God is love.

May we all remember that in the moment that you activate the knowing and remembrance of the primary axiom of creation “as it is within, so it is without.” At that precise moment, without a shadow of a doubt, you will remember that Mother-Father God, our almighty creator, has created it so that your perfect divine mate exists in this realm, at this time, in order for you to successfully fulfill the promise you made at the time of Lemuria. To come back together, in eternal and sacred union, on both the inner and the outer planes of consciousness.

Twin Flames and their Role in the Ascension.

I was shown by my spirit team that every time a Twin Flame pair individuate and go off on their own individual journey and then reunite again, the momentum of this reunion is so immense that it literally births a brand new star and the star's name is a combination of you and your Twin Flame.

My spirit team went out of their way to show me the extraordinary glory that is activated on a spiritual level every time a Twin Flame pair comes back into Union, whether that be on the inner planes of consciousness or the outer planes of consciousness.

The momentum of this reunion is so extraordinary, that the energy that is released is precisely what will lift this planet from the third dimension to the fifth dimension.

I was shown that Mother-Father God has decreed a critical mass of these Twin Flame unions to align now, enabling the recognition and remembrance of the identity of many Starseeds' true divine counterpart.

Ultimately, the journey of the soul is to fully awaken to its eternal union with its own God self and as soon as that realisation is reached, the words "as it is within, so it is without" become very apparent.

It soon becomes obvious that the perfect intelligence of creation has created it such that all the codes are stored safely within you, to experience high orgasmic bliss or the inner alchemical marriage with your own self, also known as the Hieros Gamos.

This is directly connected to the sacred awakening of your own Kundalini serpents that lay dormant at the base of your spine. These are known as the masculine and feminine polarity Kundalini serpents, Ida and the Pingala.

Kundalini Energy

I would like to go further now in explaining in greater detail what I have been shown about the Kundalini energy that lies at the base of our spine.

When the Kundalini energy is dormant, this represents duality consciousness. This represents third-dimensional consciousness, separation consciousness, the idea of us, them, me and you, self and God.

Every time a soul incarnates onto the physical plane, an agreement is made on a higher level that our Kundalini energy will be dormant. At some point, on our evolutionary journey (if we are Starseeds and sign up for the full awakening process), we will experience a cosmic trigger, which will stir the Kundalini energy to come out of its comatose asleep state into its upright and awakened state.

The moment when the Kundalini energy rises, the first serpent to rise automatically activates the opposite polarity. As soon as these two polarities rise and awaken at the base of the spine, they immediately recognise each other and rush together in sacred union, remembrance and sacred marriage.

At the moment of this sacred union, which occurs at the base of the spine, the energy then rises up throughout all of the chakras. In this profound momentum, it must be noted that all manner of shadow remnants and ancestral shadow remnants that have been lurking around in one's energy centres and cells are thoroughly exposed, drawn out and ultimately released up through the spinal column.

As the Kundalini energy rises, it rises in sacred bliss and sacred union, cleaning and cleansing out and bringing light to any darkness that is held within the being.

The Kundalini awakening is an extremely confronting experience and it is something that transforms you at the deepest depths of your being.

The purpose of this chapter is to activate the DNA codes within you that are fully responsible for your own Ascension and stabilising in fifth-dimensional consciousness through the sacred inner alchemical marriage of your own masculine and feminine energy; that which is known as the Hieros Gamos.

A Further Explanation of the Kundalini Awakening

As spoken about in the last chapter, at some point on our evolutionary journey, all-star beings who have signed up to awaken on the Ascension path come to a moment whereby the Kundalini serpents, who reside at the base of the spine in a comatose state, are triggered to come out of their dormant state (which represents duality consciousness) and into their unified state, which represents the inner alchemical marriage, also known as the Hieros Gamos.

Twin Flame unions represent the death of duality consciousness, because in order for you to be in a successful and triumphant Twin Flame union, you have had to experience the Kundalini awakening and thus death of identification as a separate ego identity.

The Kundalini awakening summarised is: The initiate moves from a place where by the Kundalini serpents, at the base of the spine, are in their dormant, asleep state (which is representative of the idea or belief that one is separate from the whole and separate from God), to their merged and unified state which is symbolic of the initiate's oneness with God.

It is very important at this stage of the book that you understand that the dormant Kundalini represents duality consciousness, i.e., each of the serpents are separate from each other and the awakened Kundalini energy represents unity consciousness.

What happens in the Kundalini awakening (which is very often triggered by either meeting a Catalyst Twin, a genuine Twin or a spiritual teacher) is that the Kundalini serpents at the base of the spine experience a specific trigger, which then causes them to begin to stir after their very long slumber.

After this initial trigger one of the serpents will awaken - usually the feminine, and she immediately will recognize her divine counterpart, the masculine, whom she then goes on to prod, saying to him, "Wake up, wake up, wake up." In the moment they both rise, their eyes lock, and they then rush towards each other in sacred and perpetual recognition and union.

In that moment of the union of the masculine and feminine energies within the base of the spine, also known as the Ida and the Pingala, this represents the sacred marriage. This represents oneness. This represents wholeness. This represents that which perceived itself as separate and dualistic coming back home to itself and making a whole circle again.

This whole circle represents the consciousness of oneness, which is non-dualistic consciousness. We are awakened to the knowing and the remembrance, that who I am is one with all of creation. I am not a separate drop of water, separate from every other drop of water. Who I am is the whole, entire ocean. Who you are is the whole, entire ocean!

Your ego consciousness would have you believe that you are a separate identity, but that is because your egoic consciousness is calibrated for the third-dimensional illusion. And it is the third-dimensional illusion which has kept the planet entrapped within the lower dimensional realms.

The reason why Twin Flames are so crucial for the Ascension of Mother Gaia is that Twin Flames have experienced a genuine, bona fide spiritual awakening. And as we all know, the macro is a reflection of the micro and the fruit of an awakened Twin Flame unit is the highest vibrational frequency that exists within the universe.

When you awaken spiritually, this means that you experience the marriage, the internal marriage, of your own divine masculine and feminine energies within. And this is why I am often guided to speak about the Heiros Gamos, the Kundalini awakening, the inner alchemical marriage. Because this is what the entire awakening is about.

This marriage, this internal marriage of your own Kundalini energy, is also a mirror of the marriage of the divine self with Mother-Father God. When your divine self has awoken from the dualistic matrix consciousness to the knowing and the remembrance of its eternal self - its divine self, when you've experienced the marriage of the Kundalini energy within the base of your own spine, this then activates the eternal remembrance of the sacred marriage of the divine self with God. And it is in this marriage with the self and Mother-Father God all suffering is removed for eternity.

Every time a soul chooses to incarnate on the earthly realm, an agreement is made on a higher spiritual level that our soul consciousness would drop in vibrational density, to a level whereby it can co-exist and blend into the third-dimensional matrix field.

Every soul agrees that when we incarnate, our Kundalini energy will be dormant/asleep at the base of our spine, awaiting the moment of a preordained cosmic trigger, that will ultimately awaken both serpents out of their dormant state.

When the Kundalini energy is asleep and comatose at the base of the spine, this represents caterpillar consciousness. This represents duality consciousness. This represents third-dimensional consciousness. The idea of separation: us and them, me and you, my land, your land, ownership and control.

Symptoms of Kundalini awakening are: a powerful release of unconditional love, as well as the sensation of being continuously bathed in a stream of angelic downloads that wash over us, cleaning and transmuting everything that is not love.

Extraordinary Experience of Spiritual Awakening

When the Kundalini energy, that has unified and merged at the base of the spine, merges with the heart chakra, this brings with it an ecstatic release of bliss as we awaken and remember our divine heritage and our divine identity that is our birthright.

As the Kundalini energy continues to rise, cleaning out and cleansing all of the chakra systems, it reaches the third eye centre. This could be very much likened to a windscreen wiper cleaning very misty and sticky windows. This is an extraordinarily powerful experience, as you literally feel that your sight is being cleansed and purified from the very core of your being. This results in us becoming extremely psychic and gifted, when it comes to being able to read our Brothers and Sisters and the issues that they are experiencing from a higher soul perspective.

It is also worth noticing at this point that during this stage of the Kundalini awakening, very often we become extremely magnetic to children and animals and everyone who is holding a stabilised high vibration.

As the energy continues to rise, it merges with our crown centre and activates an opening of the crown seal. This then creates a circular flow of energy from the base to the crown. In that moment, one has the experience and the irrefutable knowing that the circle within is complete.

One realises as the Kundalini energy reaches the crown centre, that this is when we become one with our creator self, with our God self, our higher self. The energy then begins to circulate within our own energetic field from the base to the crown and so on…

The momentum of this flow of circular energy brings forth with it extremely high, rapturous, ecstatic, blissful, orgasmic frequencies and codes, which are then subsequently released from the sacral area.

This process that is being spoken about here is the personal and individual Ascension process. This is because one's consciousness is married and merged at the base of the spine and one experiences the ensuing ascent of the Kundalini energy from the base to the crown. This activates the connection or indeed circular motion (you could say) within one's own higher self and earthly self.

This represents union and marriage on all levels, and on all planes of consciousness, because at this moment, the soul remembers its union with its eternal divine self, and the soul remembers its union with God. Indeed, the soul remembers at this point its union with all that is and all that has ever been and all that ever will be.

This experience of all knowing, of deep and abiding Gnosis, entirely removes and collapses all lower timelines that were linked to the false belief of duality and separation. And in this experience, the soul truly ascends from third-dimensional consciousness to fifth-dimensional consciousness.

Because fifth-dimensional consciousness represents unity consciousness and the third dimension represents separation and duality consciousness, the Ascension of the soul is from duality - separation consciousness - to unity and sacred marriage. Or, in other words, from third-dimensional consciousness to fifth-dimensional consciousness.

Ascension of One's Consciousness and the Pineal Gland

Thus, the Ascension of one's consciousness is the knowing and the remembrance that I am an eternal being. And that I am in eternal union with the creator of all that is. This means that I've got guardian angels, I've got a spirit team that's watching over me. I've got my beloveds that have crossed over to the other side that are also acting as spirit guides. It means that you are not alone. It means you are safe. It means you are protected.

We are so protected, Brothers and Sisters; but most cannot see this, as we have all been programmed so heavily by the third-dimensional matrix…

The Ascension of one's consciousness is hugely connected to the third eye opening and this is directly connected to the Kundalini energy, the sacred merge of the Kundalini, at the base of the spine.

Once this merge takes place and the Kundalini serpents travels up through the spine, this opens up the third eye centre and activates codes in the pineal gland.

According to esoteric teachings, there is a sacred fluid produced in a small thin layer of grey matter found in each cerebral hemisphere that is located just above our ears. These two thin nerve layers are called "claustrum."

The pineal gland is considered the male organ and is thus electrical in nature. The pituitary gland is considered feminine in nature and is thus considered magnetic. As you can see here in this general explanation, everything comes down to the sacred union of the masculine and feminine, the magnetic and the electrical.

Within the sacred journey of this fluid, it flows down from the claustrum, then separates, and then part of it splits and goes into the pineal gland and the other part goes into the pituitary body.

The pineal gland (male) gives it electrical properties, whilst the pituitary gland (female) gives it magnetic properties.

The Bible makes reference to the land of milk and honey and some scholars believe that this is referencing the pineal gland secretions, which are yellow and the pituitary gland secretions, which are white.

This area, known as the Eye of Horus, was very important to ancient Egyptians, as when these different secretions flow down from the two glands, they flow down the spine through the semilunar ganglia and at the solar plexus they produce a seed.

This process was known as internal salvation. This place is called "Bethlehem," which is a house of bread, where Christ was born. Jesus also called himself the "bread of life. Humans start producing the seed in this area from around the age of twelve, when puberty starts.

Israel is promised, the return to the land of milk and honey. It is told in the Bible and in esoteric terms, this references the return of the seed to the area in the brain where those two secretions – white and golden – are produced. This seed, anointed by the oil of the spinal cord, then travels upwards and is crucified at "Golgotha" – also known as the skull. This ensures this process causes the renewal of the mind and the transformation of the body to a higher vibration.

This is one of the most extraordinary alchemies that exists in creation.

This is a vast and complex subject, which I am simply touching upon here. And I can only really hope to deliver you some aspects of this huge subject matter. However, the message I am getting from spirit is that the fact that we are having this conversation is extremely powerful and is triggering very old soul memories within you.

The truth is we are all the carriers of this ancient knowledge, this ancient truth. Within our own heart lies the sacred scriptures and these words that are being very carefully chosen by spirit, are being sent forth to assist you with light, in order to trigger your own awakening, so that your consciousness can be flooded with the knowing and remembrance that indeed you are a multi-dimensional avatar being.

It is so essential now that everyone awakens in order to experience the inner marriage with their eternal divine beloved, who actually resides in their own Kundalini energy.

One of the most extraordinary, profound realisations I have experienced on my spiritual path is the fact that my Twin Flame is the masculine Kundalini serpent who resides at the base of my spine. And I am the feminine Kundalini serpent who resides at the base of my beloved's spine.

Rumi was absolutely right when he said:

The minute I heard my first love story,

I started looking for you,

not knowing how blind that was.

Lovers don't finally meet somewhere,

they're in each other all along

The whole point is to awaken and activate the codes of the internal marriage, as this is what activates and awakens the third eye.

When you are in your awakened state, your vibration has automatically shifted from being calibrated towards the third-dimensional, matrix illusion. Suddenly you are the rebel and have broken free from all those limited programmes that the third dimension was imposing upon you. At this stage you have fully awoken from the illusion, that you are a victim, to the realization that 'who I am is a co-creator, a vast eternal, magical being with zero limits.'

With this comes the full Awakening to the remembrance that there are no limits in my consciousness, except the ones that I believe. And, my job now, as an awakened being, is to keep clearing those false limited beliefs.

The Caterpillar and Butterfly Analogy

The perfect analogy to explain the transformation of one's consciousness from the third dimension to the fifth dimension is the journey the caterpillar goes on to become the butterfly.

The caterpillar represents the potential of the butterfly but it is encased in a vibration of perceived limitation, until at a certain moment upon its evolutionary trajectory, the metamorphic transformational process is triggered.

Prior to that moment, the caterpillar appears to be locked into a limited vibrational reality, but of course, nothing could be further from the truth.

This is a perfect analogy to explain the evolutionary process.

Do you ever feel a sense of limitation? If so, this is due to the programming of the third dimension. In truth, you hold the potential and the seeds within you to be fully and completely liberated and to transform from a third dimensional, dualistically, orientated person/caterpillar, to a fifth-dimensional, 100% liberated butterfly.

As the caterpillar resides within its third-dimensional limited form for a set amount of time, at some point within its evolutionary trajectory, the transformational process is triggered and the caterpillar literally embarks on a dying process, whereby it de-materialises itself and becomes a liquid goo in order for the liquid light to create those exquisite butterfly wings.

For those of us on the Ascension path, this dying experience and returning to goo can be very much related to us transcending the need for other people's approval.

On the Ascension path we quickly understand that a lot of our Brothers and Sisters are very much at peace with being asleep to the glaringly obvious display of divinity that stares us all all in the face, in every second of our existence. So many of our brothers and sisters are locked into the third-dimensional matrix thought grid. And therefore, it becomes glaringly apparent that we must not seek our stability or sense of wellbeing from needing asleep people's approval or indeed any person's approval.

I remember that I have made an agreement with Mother-Father God who is watching over me, that every single minute, of every single day, I will aspire to be the best Daughter that I can possibly be. And therefore, I do not need to seek other people's approval, as the only approval I ever need is Mother-Father God’s.

I hope and pray that these words are bringing clarity to you and activating lightbulb moments for you. Essentially this is what I have found to be the main issue, that is completely eradicated when we transform from a third-dimensional caterpillar to a fifth-dimensional butterfly. We completely transcend the need for another person's approval and this is replaced by an incessant need to please God, our creator, and a need to be of endless and continual service to our Brothers and Sisters.

Power and Potency of Unconditional Love

On one's spiritual and evolutionary path, that we will have designed and co-created at the feet of our creator, Mother-Father God, prior to our incarnation, it is pre-arranged that certain key trigger moments will be encoded to time-release at specific points on our evolutionary trajectory, in order to activate and trigger our Kundalini energy to come out of its dormant state and into its active and awakened state.

Each of us makes a contract between Mother-Father God and our higher selfto experience certain key trigger moments on our evolutionary Ascension path, whereby our dormant Kundalini energy will be activated so that it may awaken and rise, enabling us to come home to God consciousness.

As soon as these two Kundalini energies awaken at the base of the spine, this merge activates the initiate's experience of the inner alchemical marriage, also known as the Hieros Gamos.

As I mentioned earlier, due to the intense false programming of the third dimension, my spirit team has guided me to repeat important spiritual truths in various different ways and from various different angles in order to act as an antidote to the false programming of the third dimension.

It bears repeating that an extraordinarily powerful momentum is activated when this sacred reunion occurs at the base of the spine between the masculine and feminine Kundalini serpents.

As this Merger takes place the two entwined energies begin their ascent, or you could say, their rise, throughout all of the chakra systems in the body.

As this energy moves through the chakra systems, it cleans and cleanses and brings a very much needed light to many of the sticky, dark shadow aspects lurking within the unconscious realms.

In this momentum of the sacred union of the Kundalini energy rising up the spine, at some point it connects with the heart consciousness.

As the Kundalini energy merges with the heart chakra, it activates an extraordinary release of sacred codes that are associated with unconditional love - the love of our eternal creator. This is because the heart is the central chakra in the system and is the place within us where heaven and Earth meet.

Once these codes are experienced by the heart chakra, this activates an extraordinary release of memories that are associated with sacred marriage and divine love; memories that have been stored within the heart chakra since time immemorial.

How Does One Reach the Zero-Point Field?

Let us now spend some of our time together discussing how we arrive home to the Zero-point field of consciousness.

In order to reach the Zero-point field of consciousness, you must commit to a spiritual practice. You must take responsibility for your consciousness and realise that if you do not take the reins of your consciousness - your ego will.

This is the first and fundamental step in reaching the Zero-point field. The second is to realise that we are here on this Earth to serve our Brothers and Sisters. Particularly if you are feeling down or sad, it is a very good idea to think about something that you can do for somebody else and actually go out of your way to do it. This is the quickest and fastest way to lift your vibration.

If you commit to a practice such as this very quickly, your vibration will stabilize at a high level.

In order to come to the Zero-point field, you have to have practices that you are doing regularly. This is not a one hit wonder, a "do it one time" meditation, whereby you learn a technique and boom, that's it, you've arrived! This is a practice that requires a full commitment from you for the rest of your life.

I would like to now share with you some more potent ways to attain stabilisation within the Zero-field of consciousness.

One of the most powerful and potent ways to reach the Zero-point field of consciousness is through the remembrance and activation of the sacred union or the Hieros Gamos, within one's own self. This then very often activates the recognition of one's own divine counterpart, on the outer plane of consciousness.

Once this occurs, this then opens up codons within your soul and your DNA to bring online downloads of information from the Akashic fields about your entire soul's journey.

As this information becomes available to you, it becomes very apparent that certain traumatic events occurred within certain timelines (related to persecution, betrayal, abandonment, isolation and much, much more). And as one who has reached and attained eternal abiding and resting in the Zero-point field remembers, it is our sacred duty to go forth as the multi-dimensional medicine man or woman that we truly are, to re-meet those timelines in order to re-correct them, heal them, and ultimately bring a quantum healing balm to those traumatic experiences, in order to activate an unfreezing of the hitherto, previously frozen aspect of our consciousness.

In my accompanying workbook that goes along with this book I have brought through a number of extremely powerful and unique quantum healing modalities that will assist you to achieve profound and miraculous transformation on so many levels, especially when you work with the alchemy of this book. My heart knows that this is a truly powerful sacred offering, that is shifting the consciousness of everyone who holds these sacred words in their hand.

I often work with the extremely powerful technique of quantum time travel called QTTT, an extremely powerful and transformative healing modality that I was privileged to bring to the world.

This is a phenomenal Ascension tool in the great toolbox of gifts our creator has given us that assists us to go back and forth to work with any timeline that we intend to transform; that we may for once and for all release the trauma and the blocks that have been stored there, in some cases, for eons.

Trauma and blocks can often be likened to ice blocks, occurring within one's own energetic field throughout one's evolutionary process. These blocks are caused by traumatic incidents which create patterns of 'stuckness' in our physical and emotional fields, forming illnesses and addictions. It quickly becomes apparent, as we go forth as the multi-dimensionally awakened beings that we are, bringing healing and medicine balm to those timelines, and it is in fact possible to unfreeze those frozen parts.

We quickly see that when we release these blocks, we release vast amounts of power from our soul consciousness that previously had been stuck, which results in Chi energy now clearing and being able to move freely.

All of this deep transformational timeline work is connected to our Shadow aspect, which I will speak about in much greater depth in the upcoming chapters.

Once that Chi energy has been cleared, it gives us a greater level of spiritual power, radiance and charisma, and makes you extremely magnetic to all benevolent energies.

When one arrives home in the Zero-point field of consciousness, there is an eternal expansion into greater and greater levels of awareness and a direct experience of that.

CHAPTER NINE - ZERO-POINT FIELD OF CONSCIOUSNESS AND TIMELINES

One of the most astounding things I realised when I experienced the Ascension of my consciousness was that in the Zero-point field of consciousness all timelines operate concurrently. All timelines run in unison and parallel to the present moment.

This means that via our consciousness, we are able to access past, present, future and concurrent timelines. We can access the timeline of Atlantis. We can access the timeline of Lemuria. We can access the timeline of the moment of creation. There is no limit to the timeline's past, present, future or current that we can experience via our own consciousness; our own imagination.

In our individual consciousness, we can attune to the timeline of our future, timelines in a thousand years, a million years - past, present, concurrent or future.

All of this information has remained a mystery until now, but the truth is that it is directly through our own consciousness that we attune to the different dimensional realms of reality.

All dimensional realms of consciousness are able to be activated within the Zero-point field, within the present moment and when you arrive home in the present moment, you fully remember that you are a multi-dimensional avatar being.

Through that remembrance, you remember that your consciousness is automatically attuned to all of the higher dimensional realms of consciousness simply through a choice. And through you literally choosing or indeed tuning into those higher dimensional realms of consciousness, you are able to directly interface with all dimensional realms of consciousness.

Imagination is Directly Linked to the Mind of God

When I awakened to the truth of who I am, I very, very quickly remembered that the imagination, my imagination, is directly linked to the mind of God and that God, the infinite creator, communicates to all of us through the sacred marriage of our heart consciousness and our imagination.

In this remembrance true abiding liberation was born and I was no longer a slave to my imaginative faculties. No longer an asleep person, constantly being steered by my egoic consciousness into illusionary experiences of victimhood, pain and separation. I was now blessed with the innate knowing that my higher self had taken full control of the reins and was steering my lower earthly self, to become one with my higher self.

In my Ascension experience, my higher self had fully taken over the reins. And from this moment on, I understood that it was my absolute duty to navigate and visit timelines, whereby certain blissful and certain traumatic experiences had happened to me on a personal level; that I may clear the stuck energy within those traumatic timelines and access future timelines, whereby I am in high-dimensional states of consciousness, having manifested particular dreams and visions that I have held dear to me in my heart.

I remembered so much about the power of the imagination with regards to sending forth direct instructions into the consciousness matrix of all that is.

Our imagination is directly linked to the super consciousness of every soul, every being alive and when we work with symbology which is the language of the imagination, we deeply utilise the powerful force of our subconscious mind, which is linked to the subconscious mind of everyone and all that is.

It is much more powerful to manifest something from the unseen realm into the seen realm, when we work with the powerful tools of visualisation and Symbology which are directly linked to the imagination which, ultimately in its purest form, truly is the mind of God.

When the Circle is Complete

I would love now to share with you what I have been shown by my higher self team.

As I have mentioned before, I do not share any regurgitated information that I have gathered from books. Every single thing I share is what I have experienced directly from my own internal Gnosis.

And what I have experienced is that when you experience the Hieros Gamos - the inner alchemical merge with your own divine sacred Kundalini energy, your own divine self and God - when you experience this sacred union, you arrive home in the Zero-point field of consciousness; a place where you unequivocally and irrefutably experience the vibrational knowing that the circle within yourself is complete.

At that moment of recognition of your internal completion, this activates the sacred marriage, the sacred and eternal union of self with God. You then entirely transcend the third-dimensional matrix and transcend the confusion of the fourth-dimensional matrix realm, that is still somewhat hijacked by the energies of duality. At this point your soul has come home to itself and this is symbolised by the snake eating his own tail - making the full circle.

As soon as you come to this plateau of vibrational completion, this activates all of the codes, or indeed the codons in your DNA, that enable you to transition from the lower dimensional realms of consciousness to the blissful rainbow crystalline unicorn-filled realm of the fifth dimension. This is the plateau one's consciousness arrives at, just after the fourth dimension, where you truly, truly arrive home in unity consciousness.

So, may it be reiterated again and again: Unity consciousness is the Zero-point field. It is the place where God consciousness is "I am that I am"…there is nothing, but "I am that I am" within the Zero-point field, there is only God consciousness. There is no duality in fifth-dimensional consciousness, which is pure ecstatic, sacred and eternal joy and union.

The entry point to the fifth dimension is through the Zero-point field and one arrives at the Zero-point field through the heart, through the sacred inner alchemical marriage of your own Kundalini energy, the Hieros Gamos.

It Constantly Bears Repeating to Awaken from the Lies

As you arrive home in the Zero-point field of consciousness, you remember that you are an avatar being and you remember many of the timelines that you have existed in, including the timeline of Atlantis. You remember the timeline of Lemuria, you remember your galactic origins. You remember that you have an eternal connection to your galactic origins. You remember that your soul is so vast, that you are very possibly more likely living concurrent lifetimes; for example, as a Pleiadian, Sirian, or as a LYRAN being.

It must be repeated here that the fifth dimension is the gateway to multiple-dimensional consciousness; sixth-dimensional, seventh-dimensional, eighth-dimensional and above. The fifth dimension is where one arrives at unity consciousness, and the above dimensions are simply a deepening and expansion into greater levels of union with God...

As soon as you arrive at fifth-dimensional consciousness, all that was hidden to you becomes available once again.

As you arrive home in the Zero-point field or fifth dimensional consciousness, all remembrances are fully activated with regards to your power to direct the God-given light with your sacred energy, to re-correct any timeline.

That is why I speak so much about the timelines, particularly the timeline of Atlantis and the importance of the Twin souls going back to the time of Atlantis, to re-correct and restore that timeline so that this original core separation did not occur.

As soon as we are awake, we truly remember that it is our duty and responsibility as avatar beings to create brand-new timelines whenever we wish.

CHAPTER TEN - SHADOW WORK

I am being directed by the spirit of this book to speak now about the extremely important subject matter that is shadow work.

The shadow refers to that which is hidden, that which is unconscious. Very often it is not until we are triggered that we have any idea what our shadow issues really are. The shadow self in truth represents the fragmented, traumatized parts of the self that have separated and frozen from the whole.

Every time we ignore or deny an unintegrated fragmented aspect of our beautiful divine self, we invariably lose vital energy.

And until the work is done, whereby we stand underneath that shadow aspect and hold space for it and listen attentively to what it has to say…then and only then does the alchemy take place and we transform the shadow from darkness to light - FROM LEAD TO GOLD.

Every time we do that, we claim deeper and deeper levels of vitality from our soul consciousness. This then activates our higher self to send forth greater levels of energy to be dispensed, now that there are zero blocks restricting the flow of this naturally high energy.

I feel, myself, I have always been very brave when it comes to facing parts of myself that could be defined as shadow aspects.

As I progressed further along my spiritual path, it became apparent to me that life could be likened to a game of Pac-Man. We are all on a particular level of a Pac-Man game and as we move around and progress on that level, we encounter golden stars.

What I have discovered on my journey is that these golden stars can be likened to our shadow self.

As we encounter a particular level of the Pac-Man game and come across the golden stars, we are each presented with a choice - do we try to avoid the golden star by ignoring it and pretending it's not there, or do we stand underneath it?

By using this metaphor of a Pac-Man game, I would like to explain what I have been shown by my spiritual Ascension team, and this is that the shadow self is often the wounded child aspect which has remained ignored or denied for quite some time.

I have been shown that as we encounter those golden stars which represent our shadow aspect, if we can approach these aspects with respect, attention and inner standing, we can literally stand under this aspect of our self and give it the attention that it needs.

This integrates us on a very deep level and it brings us back home to wholeness, back home to our divine, eternal self.

If we approach the shadow aspect in this manner, I have discovered that what occurs is a profound up-levelling of our frequency. We literally go to the next level of the Pac-Man game; the next level vibrationally, of our experience of being alive.

However, if we do not deal with our shadow aspect in this wise and mature way, then we stay stuck on that level until we can face this aspect, integrate it and bring it home.

I have brought through an extremely powerful chapter in my accompanying workbook that goes along with this chapter that will help you have a direct experience of working with and deeply healing your wounded child/ shadow aspect.

I really hope that this analogy makes sense to you all. It has helped me enormously understand the imperativeness of appreciating all the moments we get triggered. These are a sacred opportunity for us to integrate a somewhat separated aspect of ourselves that is desperately needing to come back home to wholeness and integration with our divinity.

If we do not have the tools or the skills to be able to meet our shadow self in a way that will initiate a deep healing, transformation and integration, then it is not possible for us to go further along on that particular level of life or indeed the Pac-Man game.

Therefore, I have discovered that, as I willingly embrace the fact that I will be triggered on this path and there is a strong likelihood that experiences of competitiveness, jealousy, unresolved anger, unworthiness and betrayal will at some point be triggered on my individual awakening path...

I have come home to the realisation that this is indeed a gift and this gift shows me a part of myself that I am very probably in denial about, or that I am holding guilt and shame towards, an aspect which is now ready to be integrated and brought home.

As I go forward and experience these triggers, I have learned that this is a wonderful and powerful opportunity for me to stop and say thank you, as an opportunity for extreme and profound growth has presented itself at my door.

Solutions to Working with Shadow Aspects

I would like to now speak about the incredibly powerful healing modality that I have brought through called QTTT.

QTTT is a healing modality which works as a quantum time travel technique.

In this powerful, sacred work, we identify the unhealed, frozen aspects of the child self that have experienced great trauma.

We access that timeline via the future self of the individual; i.e., we send the future self of the traumatised person back to the timeline whereby they received the traumatic imprint and through the act of the future self, meeting and holding space - standing under and validating the experiences of the traumatised aspect. This is what creates the alchemy of healing and transformation.

It is such a powerful healing modality and without doubt is the most powerful healing modality I have ever used. This is why I was guided to train facilitators to work with this process, as it can definitely be considered a Maha/Mother healing process.

The results are extraordinarily powerful and profound.

People experience the clearing of long-term health issues and long-term emotional issues, but mostly people come home to themselves and realise that they are the one that they have been searching for and praying for.

Whilst society would have everyone believe it's a Twin Flame or a Guru that you are searching for, truly all we are searching for is our own parental self to step forward to heal us and re-correct any traumatic incidents that took place in any timeline that we have experienced.

Please see the back of the book for more information on the QTTT training programs that I will be hosting once a year.

The feedback that I have received from all of the facilitators is so powerful. People have experienced such extraordinary healing miracles from working with this technique.

The reason I am sharing this in this chapter is because I have devoted the last few paragraphs to speaking about the intensity and importance of doing shadow work and this modality offers an extremely profound re-correction and healing towards our shadow aspect, bringing us truly home to our divine self.

The Alchemy of the Soul

On my journey I have discovered that if I truly have the courage to stop and be grateful for any trigger and understand that it is connected to an oftentimes unconscious part of myself, which has either separated or is frozen on some timeline in my energetic field. When I meet this trigger or this shadow aspect in gratitude and stand underneath this shadow aspect, in order to hold space for it, as though it were a very wounded, sad child…I have learned that when I do that, when I extend a deep arm of compassion towards this somewhat separated aspect of myself, I then go onto experience the alchemy of my soul.

In many ways it could be perceived as though the shadow aspect represents the lead of one's consciousness, the separate, egoic belief system.

I have found that through standing under, holding space and listening to this aspect, I have had many, many direct experiences of this causing and activating an extraordinary alchemy within my own personal soul's consciousness, whereby the lead of the shadow self transforms.

Through facing one's own rejected shadow aspect and bringing it home to the unconditional love of the parental self or higher self, this very act transforms the shadow which represents the lead-based, egoic consciousness into the gold of the Christed self.

This is a most wondrous experience to behold and comes back to the great analogy of the Pac-Man game. When one truly understands the importance of how to work with the shadow aspect, which has presented on this particular level of one's evolutionary sojourn, as soon as one truly does the alchemical work that we have just spoken about, then one truly and absolutely transcends to the next level of their evolutionary trajectory.

Impersonal Aspects of the Shadow Self

The shadow aspects we experience are very often not personal to us and are directly related to our ancestral lineages and thought forms in the Collective.

Very often we will take on the shadow patterns of our parents, particularly our same-sex parents. We will take on these patterns and these programs as our own and these false, limited beliefs will create thought forms which will go on to create experiences which are a direct manifestation and reflection of that thought form.

Many of the shadow aspects of our consciousness are also related to the collective. We are all one consciousness, ultimately under a spell of separation. However, nothing could be further from the truth.

All that exists is Mother-Father God consciousness, which is an eternal diamond fractal of light, and we are all perfect offspring of that great prismic diamond light. And due to the irrevocable fact that we are all One, this means that on some level we are all connected to all thought forms.

Very often the shadow aspects that we incarnate to transmute are stored within the collective consciousness and the brave souls that we are, we very often step forward and sign up for that role to clear a particular thought form for the collective, in the current incarnation that we are in.

I hope these words inspire you to rejoice the next time you get triggered and understand that within you is most likely a frozen or separate aspect of yourself which is calling out for integration; and that you will see that this person or this situation has been sent by God in order to help you recognize the vibration of this hidden part of yourself. So that you may respond in a different way from how you have usually responded in the past, to this aspect of yourself, which has very often been denied, projected upon and thoroughly rejected…

Each time we get triggered, we are being presented with an opportunity to approach an unintegrated aspect of our psyche in a new and refreshing manner, that we may learn the lesson, embrace the shadow self, and ultimately transcend to the next level of consciousness.

I sincerely hope that this chapter has inspired you to remember and understand that you are not alone and you are certainly not unique, in the sense that everybody who incarnates into the third dimension has a shadow self.

Another reason we are all riddled with shadow aspects is because of the fact that our soul consciousness drops in density to come into a physical earthly incarnation. Everybody has to experience a drop in the density of their soul frequency. In order for us to do that, we very often will take on issues or programmes of the third dimension that will enable us to acclimatise to the third-dimensional reality matrix.

It is highly recommended that you focus on identifying your shadow aspects and realise that there are most likely aspects of your consciousness that are feeling quite separate from your innermost being.

It is highly recommended that you identify your individual shadow aspects and call them home, one by one. Stand underneath them and listen to their story without identifying with their story and without identifying with the victim narrative.

When you do this, you grow exponentially - spiritually- and you become a force of great power, magnetism and goodness in the world.

In my humble opinion, unless you have done an extensive amount of shadow work on yourself and consider yourself to be on the spiritual path, you will always seem to be fake and inauthentic to those people on the path that have been doing the shadow work.

That is because sensitive people are able to pick up on disassociated parts of the psyche and we are intuitively able to understand that this person has not fully integrated yet.

This is not a judgment. This is simply an observation. These types of people can come across as extremely fake and inauthentic, especially if you bypass the shadow work and jump straight to affirmations and positive mindset.

Whenever we do that, we are simply pulling the rug up and stuffing all of our unconscious shadow issues underneath it; and whenever we do that, the issues always grow, until eventually they become unmanageable or turn into a chronic disease or illness.

If you have been vibrationally drawn to these words, I highly recommend keeping up to date with your shadow work. Please know that it is always advisable for you to lift up the carpet and name and claim the aspects of yourself that have appeared to be separate.

Whenever we stand underneath and identify these aspects, ultimately, we bring them home to the wholeness of our eternal being.

For many of us, there is a deep feeling of wanting to go home, which very often lives within the shadow self and that can oftentimes get triggered by pieces of music, art or poetry. These can trigger that feeling of missing home - which for some, can highlight a shadow issue of not belonging.

Many people have this issue, but they do not face this and shine a light on it. Instead, they try to suppress this issue and try to get on with their life, ignoring the fact that they don't feel like they belong.

At the back of this book, I will offer you the opportunity to work with many of the powerful MP3s that I have brought through that have assisted many people to integrate their shadow and unite with their Twin Flame on the inner and outer planes of consciousness.

CHAPTER ELEVEN - BOUNDARIES

I have created this book as a sacred offering to ultimately share with everyone the tools I have discovered that have enabled me to stabilise in fifth-dimensional consciousness since 2013.This is a powerful sacred space that has been created in order for me to share all of the downloads I have received about the importance of Twin Flames - the Kundalini awakening, the Hieros Gamos - and how all of that directly relates to the great Awakening and the Ascension of Mother Gaia.

However, it is not possible for me to speak about these two subjects without speaking in depth about the tools that will enable all of you readers to fully, once and for all, activate the self-mastery codes within your DNA so that you may become one with your higher self and do the final flip from caterpillar to butterfly consciousness.

Please know that the intention behind every word that is written in this sacred text is deeply encoded with the intention for you to fully awaken in this moment, to the remembrance that you are a glorious and innocent child of the universe, a descendant of Mother-Father God - the holiest of the holies. You carry the Royal blood lineage, as do all of Mother-Father God's children; we are all special in the eyes of our creator.

The intention of this book is to activate and remind you of your perpetual innocence and empowerment as a creator, so that the frequencies of the words on this page may fully awaken you out of the Quagmire of the illusions of the third dimension, which has sought to cast a spell over your angelic consciousness.

This is a wake-up call of the highest order

Brothers and Sisters.

We each have a responsibility to be guardian of our precious child self, our divine child self. And we do that by having vigilant boundaries and not allowing toxic energy into our sacred space. This is one of the most powerful ways that you can become a master of self-love - by remembering at all times that you are a precious child of God and you deserve to be loved.

You do not deserve to be judged or criticised or hurt in any way and if that energy is coming into your field, it is your duty and responsibility to say a very firm 'NO' and to set your boundaries, to ensure that you are protected at all times and your beautiful inner child is safe.

A person who truly loves themselves sets very clear and vigilant boundaries towards the energy that they will allow into their sacred, sexual, energetic space. Through one's own love towards oneself, one automatically teaches everyone around us how to treat us and how to love us.

Indeed, all of our relationships are a reflection of the relationship that we have with ourselves; when we have finally arrived at the place of recognition of our true value and our true worth - which we remember is something that we must claim and not something that the world will willingly give us.

Once this has fully claimed, then once again we reach the place within our evolutionary trajectory whereby the circle is complete and a new level of mastery in this area of our life is attained.

We go to the next level, and we also teach everyone in our reality exactly how to treat us, especially within our sacred relationships, and this is to treat us with honour, respect and remembrance of our shared divinity at all times.

We experience so many gifts when we commit to having clear and vigilant boundaries.

One thing I have noticed as a divine feminine, who has had very strong vigilant boundaries for quite some time now, is that it definitely inspires other divine feminines to speak up and also set clear boundaries.

Somehow, we are all igniting and inspiring each other to finally say no! This is a programme, an old programme that is no longer acceptable to us awakened divine feminines and it all stops here and ends here!!!

In my upcoming book "No More Crumbs" I will be speaking in great detail about the role of the divine feminine with regards to the Ascension of humanity but I definitely would like to say a few words here.

There is a reason why the divine feminine has been suppressed for millennia and that is because she is the multi-dimensional portal on Earth. She is the gateway that births spirits and she is the one that Mother-Father God has chosen for this role.

The reason why the divine feminine has been given this role, is because she is deemed less corruptible than the divine masculine.

This truth is depicted in all of the mythical teachings, particularly in the original Tarot.

The divine feminine energy is "knowing - intuition - gnosis - wisdom - insight - clairvoyance and clairaudience" with the predominant gift of the divine feminine, being that she is deeply tapped into the unseen realms of consciousness. This means that she is able to become one with her multi-dimensionality, with greater ease, as soon as she connects to her heart centre.

The wisdom of the divine feminine has been suppressed for aeons now, as the divine feminine is the gateway to God consciousness.

The divine feminine energy exists within men and women and it is so important now that men as well as women start empowering the energy of the divine feminine codes within them. Here I am referring to intuition - inner knowing, trusting one's heart consciousness, et cetera.

There are so many incredible women that have been devoting every moment of their existence to awakening spiritually and there is a deep prayer in the spiritual community for the Brothers to level up and match the divine feminines' spiritual commitment and wisdom.

I have been very strongly guided by spirit to launch a brand-new podcast titled "Where Are All The Awakened Men?" with a red cross on the W to read "Here Are All The Awakened Men." It will be a regular podcast, which I do hope you will tune in to. I will be interviewing some incredibly powerfully aligned and enlightened divine masculines. I will have some very deep conversations with them about how they got to this level, and the practices that they have committed to that have enabled them to truly stabilise in enlightened consciousness. Please visit my

website for more information
https://www.jenmccarty.co.uk

Sovereignty

On the path of spiritual awakening, at some point we all come to the realisation of our sovereignty.

Sovereignty can be quite an ambiguous subject matter, so I would just like to devote a few paragraphs to explaining what I have been shown about sovereignty.

We are each children of Mother-Father God, direct offspring of the highest creator in the universe. As such we are in direct lineage to the Royal Bloodline.

Every time a soul is born, we each have a crown that is placed and kept in our etheric field.

One of the greatest illusions of the third dimension is that there is a higher spiritual authority outside of yourself i.e., a priest or a priestess or a guru. This, though, is an allusion of the highest order, as we are in fact, all sovereign beings.

This means that every time a soul is born, Mother-Father God safely places our crown inside our energetic and etheric field, awaiting the moment of our awakening, whereby we reach into our etheric field and we firmly place our crown on our crown chakra.

In the moment that we do that, we truly and absolutely claim our sovereignty, as we are living the reality that there is no greater authority other than ourselves, who has the power to place our crown on our head.

We stand tall and proud as a child of God - that all of our Brothers and Sisters may be able to recognise their own divinity, their own sovereignty through our remembrance.

There is nothing more powerful in existence than a person who has claimed their sovereignty, a person who has remembered that they are offspring of Mother-Father God, a person who has remembered that there is no higher authority in the universe other than them.

When we place our crown on our head, we truly become one with our higher self and start accessing all the fifth-dimensional codes that are stored safely within our DNA.

If you can take away one message from this chapter, it will be that you are who you have been searching for and praying for, and you have everything that you need within you to complete your search on all planes of consciousness.

You are a divine being of the highest order and there is no higher authority than you in the universe. This is the greatest illusion of the third dimension and that is why I am repeating it over and over in this book.

This sacred text holds codes that are acting as a type of reprogramming that is the antithesis of the illusionary, third-dimensional matrix programming. Every time you remember to place your crown on your head, you offer your Brothers and Sisters a true and sincere gift of sacred remembrance and the opportunity for them to remember their perpetual and abiding divinity, as reflected in you.

CHAPTER TWELVE - SERVICE TO OTHERS

In my teachings I speak in great depth about continuously and vigilantly being in service to our Brothers and Sisters.

When one is truly awakened, it becomes a natural inevitability that we are oriented towards serving others - but we can't serve others until we love and serve our beautiful divine selves.

Until you are really there with yourself, loving yourself, having vigilant boundaries and doing the shadow work, then you're not in a position to be oriented towards service to others. So, loving oneself and serving others literally go hand in hand.

As we do this deep work of connecting with our unconscious child self, we actually experience this alchemy where we transform the wounded lead of the child self into the golden alchemy of the healed Christed self.

When we actually go through that alchemical process - the great work - the magnum opus of the soul, then we are in a position to serve our Brothers and Sisters.

The great spell of the third dimension has everyone believing that an external force is going to blast out of the higher dimensional realms and save the day. But you are the Saviour that your soul is seeking and this is the absolute truth.

When you fully and completely realise this, then naturally you will be serving your Brothers and Sisters.

I feel inspired to share with you all a story of a person that I met recently who was suffering from very deep depression and suicidal thoughts.

I said to him, after holding space and listening deeply to what he said, "Have you done anything for other people recently?" He responded, "I haven't really done anything." "Do you want to clear your depression?" "Yeah," He answered. My response was, "Then think about how you can help other people. There are seven billion people on this planet that are suffering from PTSD from being in the matrix. You could be so helpful. You could be so kind. You could be so effective, if you actually think about other people and ways that you can help them and serve them."

As I spoke these words, I witnessed a tangible difference in his demeanour and a heaviness left him. It was obvious a feeling of inspiration had entered into his field.

I could see him thinking of ways that he could apply this very powerful message from spirit.

That one conversation was enough to show me that indeed serving others is the antidote to many mental health issues, particularly depression, as when suffering from depression, one gets very lost and locked into one's own problems and identity; which in itself, is the very definition of what creates depression.

We are creator beings and we are Children of God. We are servants of divine love and as we align with our higher self, we align with the aspects that bring us bliss, wonderment, joy and even rapture…

When we are truly aligned with our higher self. When we think about other people and the ways that we can make this experience of life on Earth easier and more bearable for them. When we take actions to serve our Brothers and Sisters, this is how we lift our own vibration.

This reminds me of the saying 'you always get what you give' and I can honestly say that that is my direct experience - you do, indeed, always get what you give.

When I had that meeting with that young man after coming out of a workshop, I noticed something had definitely shifted in him. I genuinely do believe that serving others and thinking about others is the antidote to depression.

That said, you have to have that container where you understand that you are a precious divine child.

Mother-Father God gave you the job to be the parent of your child self, not your Twin Flame, not a guru, not an external teacher. You are the parent and if you can actually seal that relationship, then you're pretty much home and dry; and then it is all about service to others.

What is Self-Love

So much of my work has been focused on reminding everybody how to embody self-love. I always struggled with understanding what self-love is and what it really looks like, and I think this applies to many people in the spiritual community.

Many believe that self-love is doing lots of Yoga, repeating lots of mantras, having a vegan diet, etc., and of course that is a beautiful part of loving oneself but what I've learned on my journey is that loving oneself means actually meeting your own shadow self.

Part of the programming of the third dimension has convinced everyone that we are searching for an external teacher, a Twin flame or a guru to come along and love us for who we truly are, and this program is blocking everyone from remembering the absolute truth: That you are the one that you are searching for; YOU are the person who can resolve all of your trauma within your own energetic field.

A life-changing healing was experienced by myself when I remembered that I have a parental aspect, and I have a wounded child aspect. That I can send my parental self to my wounded child to stand underneath her and hold space for her and really, really listen to her, and check in with her, and ask her, "What is it that you need?"

When I do that, invariably she says, "I just wanted to be heard. I just wanted to be validated. I just needed you to listen to me and acknowledge me." And that's it, nothing more is needed.

This, to me, is what-self-love is. Self-love is about really being there for yourself and ceasing the addiction to endlessly project onto another person or onto something external and outside of you.

Self-love is when you are no longer convincing yourself that any external person is going to be the miracle healing balm, who will eradicate all your wounded inner child issues. We are the only ones who have the power to activate an everlasting and sincere alchemy within our soul. No one else has the power to do that.

In my accompanying workbook that goes with this book, I have brought through a chapter on self-love with exercises and meditations that will enable you to become a master very quickly of true self-love.

In Summary - What is Self-Love?

In summary, I have learned that self-love is truly identifying the lost, wounded, separated and abandoned parts of my shadow self and standing underneath them, listening to them and ultimately bringing them home to the oneness of my true self. That to me is true self-love, and how I get to have a direct living experience of loving myself, through offering unconditional love to all the different aspects of myself.

Through this amazing practice and through the many years of being committed to this practice, what very naturally comes forth from this is a very powerful ability to unconditionally love all of our Brothers and Sisters, because we truly realize that there is only oneself.

As we love our one true self and bring all the lost, abandoned and separated parts back home, we unify the fragmented ego self back into the perfect Christic structure of our original blueprint.

As this occurs, this sends out codes and ripples throughout timelines of existence that we have completed the great work of the soul - the magnum opus.

This is where we step forward as the parental self to parent the fragmented, lost, wounded shadow self, which is very often linked to our child self - as the traumas that occur ancestrally, karmically and within this lifetime, often stunt our emotional growth and evolution.

Therefore, when we do this great work of parenting the wounded shadow child self, truly this is self-love in action.

This is the work that I've been speaking about since 2013 when I experienced the full Ascension of my consciousness due to the inner alchemical merge of myself and my Twin Flame, and through this experience I understood implicitly how to work with timelines and how to heal timelines, particularly those that are entrapped in trauma and grief.

In the experience of the Ascension of my consciousness, I fully and completely came home to the remembrance that I am a multiple-dimensional avatar being and the programming of the third-dimensional matrix has sought to convince me that I am not that and that my consciousness is somehow fixed, only to the third dimension.

However, nothing could be further from the truth. I am an eternal and immortal spiritual being and my consciousness is forever linked eternally to the highest echelons of God.

I am a multiple-dimensional avatar being and my consciousness is operating concurrently on all multiple-dimensional realms of consciousness. It is through the great portal of my imagination that I link up with the mind of God and am able to visit all multiple-dimensional realms of consciousness.

It was shown to me that traversing on the higher dimensional realms of consciousness is only possible through the portal of the heart centre, which is activated through the releasing of the codes of unconditional love.

CHAPTER THIRTEEN - WHAT IS ASCENSION?

At this stage in this book's development, I feel it would be a good moment to share with you what I have been shown about Ascension and indeed, what is Ascension.

I have constantly been speaking about Ascension in this book. The very nature of this book means that the subject matter is cyclical as opposed to linear. Everything that I am sharing is coming from the Zero-point field which can be perceived as a spiral in creation, with no beginning and no end.

Firstly, I will share with you what I have been shown with regards to one’s individual personal Ascension trajectory and then what I have been shown with regards to the planet’s current collective Ascension trajectory.

Ascension is a word that explains the vibratory shift the Earth and all her inhabitants are going through from third density to fifth density.

I have been shown that the Earth matrix has been stuck or quarantined in a third-dimensional vibratory frequency range, which is somewhat connected to the choices that were made collectively and by many individuals at the time of Atlantis.

During the universal history of creation, there have been an unprecedented number of galactic wars that have taken place particularly between Orion, Andromeda and Lyra.

All of these galactic wars have contributed hugely to the circumstances the Earth matrix is currently stuck within, to this day. However, as we are now in the gateway of the great Ascension of Gaia, this is shifting and the quarantine has now been lifted. I will explain more about this later on in the chapter.

Due to this change, Earth is now moving out of a third-dimensional vibratory frequency to a fifth-dimensional, vibratory frequency band. This means that all of her children are undergoing a metamorphosis from caterpillar to butterfly consciousness, as is the Earth herself.

As the Earth descends into her fifth-dimensional glory, we will get closer and closer to the vibrations of Heaven. We will experience much more celestial light and sounds and we will be far more telepathically and psychically in tune with each other.

We will all be able to instantly heal each other, teleport and move through portals to other dimensions; not to mention all the phenomenal off-planet technology that will be made available to us such as replicators, med beds (also known as celestial healing Chambers) and travel opportunities via interdimensional portal points.

This is what we have got to look forward to, as we all fully appreciate the fact that we have the greatest seat in the house for the greatest show in the universe. I would like to share with you what I was told about the Solar flash event.

The EVENT

I had never heard of the "Event' until September 2017. On this fateful day, I went for a walk in nature near my house and as I was walking, my spirit team connected with me and shouted very loudly:

"There is going to be an event!"

I was quite shocked, as usually my spirit team spoke to me very subtly and almost silently, but this time it was loud and clear. All of a sudden, I was shown that there is a wave of light that is currently on its way and is being sent forth from Galactic Central, the central sun of our galaxy. And as this wave of light gets closer to the earthly realm, we will experience it as a pulse of light ejected out of the sun, which appears to us on Earth as a wave.

I was shown that this wave is magenta in colour and it *is* on its way from Galactic Central, but its arrival is connected to humanity's consciousness reaching a critical mass of awakened souls.

I was shown that as soon as this wave enters into Earth's atmosphere, every single person alive will feel the effects of it. It was explained to me by my spirit team that this wave is a tangible, vibratory frequency of God's presence. I was shown that as this magenta wave enters into Earth's atmosphere, it would affect everyone and there would be no one who would be unaffected by this light; that everyone who was touched by the light would have to go and lay down and assimilate the new codes and energies that are streaming forth.

I was shown that as the wave of light entered into the Earth's atmosphere and is picked up individually by humanity, this will trigger an almighty spiritual awakening for everyone.

My spirit team told me that everyone is going to awaken. All those people that are locked into the third dimension matrix, who work in banks and work in very third dimension jobs; they were all about to awaken spiritually...

My spirit team was very, very adamant that this wave is coming, that this wave is on its way. I was told that I must inform my community. I must let everyone know that I've been told about the event and that we must all prepare without delay.

As I am a musician who focuses specifically on sacred prayerful medicine music, my spirit team said to me that as soon as the wave comes and the event happens, what everyone will need is music. Spiritual music, medicine music, prayerful music. My spirit team told me that it would be highly beneficial for me to start focusing on creating music for the masses during the great spiritual awakening.

It was a very powerful message and as I said in the opening lines, very unusual for my spirit team to communicate with me in this way.

So, I walked home, and I proceeded to record a YouTube video, which you can find on my YouTube channel. I was then chatting away to my community about Twin Flames and the awakening and then all of a sudden, I remembered the message that my spirit team had brought me and so I said to everyone, "Beloveds, I just received a really important message from my spirit team and they told me that there's going to be an event." ....AND the moment that I spoke out the word "event," this huge light came into my living room and it entirely covered my face. Then, lo and behold, before I knew it, all of these light specks started dancing on the ceiling and as I was talking, this light was communicating back to me.

This was an incredibly powerful confirmation to receive from my spirit team, who were clearly aligning with the message that they had previously given me, confirming and proving that this was a genuine, bona fide message. Everyone on the video could see this play of light, these dancing light orbs that had suddenly filled up my entire room. This to me was incredible proof and validation that the message I had received was genuine.

A couple of months passed and one day I went onto Facebook to find a good friend of mine had posted:

"Has anyone heard about the event?"

Prior to that I had never heard anyone speak about the event, so I commented on her post:

"I've heard about the event."

She then proceeded to send me some videos that had been recorded, referencing the event.

Before I knew it, I found myself down an extraordinary rabbit hole, aligning with lots and lots of people, who were bringing through incredible intel and information about this so-called spiritual awakening event.

My friend's post led me to a video whereby, sadly, a woman's son had committed suicide a few years back and she was desperately trying to have a telepathic relationship with him, but to no success.

Finally, he was able to come through and transmit a message. In the message, he told her that there was going to be an event...that there was going to be a huge wave of light, coming forth from Galactic Central that was going to infuse the entire Earth consciousness and everybody would be affected by this wave of light, resulting in there being a mass spiritual awakening.

For me to come across this information was mind-blowing, as it 100% correlated with everything that my spirit team had told me.

At this point, I think it would be appropriate to remind everyone that I would never have believed there was going to be an event, unless I was told personally and individually by my spirit team. I just would never have believed it. So, to suddenly find myself being exposed to videos and people who were speaking specifically about the event, in the same way that I was shown, was very, very mind-blowing for me.

It bears mentioning here that in the Vedas the solar flash event is called the Sāṁvartaka Fire. The Vedic writings speak of rainbow coloured 'clouds' that will appear, like a rainbow display; the same as someone attaining the rainbow body.

Suffice to say I was given enough validation to know that the message that my spirit team had given me was 100% genuine.

More on the Event

So, at this point, I was well aware that there was going to be an event. There was too much evidence accruing around me, all pointing to the fact that the Earth is aligning with that which is known or that which will be remembered as "The Event." I was aware that my spirit team was wanting me to create some sort of online forum, whereby people that were interested in the event and were wanting to learn more about the event could gather.

So, one day on the 8th March 2018 (unbeknownst to me it was International Women's Day!), I was sitting with my laptop, staring at the computer screen and I thought to myself, "I'm going to create a group on Facebook. What shall I call it?"

And I decided I was going to call it "The Event Is Happening."

So, I sat there without really premeditating it at all and I created the group "The Event Is Happening." Prior to that, I had been running my global transmissions, assisting Twin Flames to come into sacred union with each other, so therefore I had built up a presence online and a small community. So, on the day that I created the group "The Event Is Happening," all of the members of my transmission groups joined, and on that first day we had at least 500 people join the group.

This created a very powerful, solid, divine feminine foundation, based on women that were really deeply doing the spiritual work to stabilize in fifth-dimensional consciousness and align with their true Twin Flame.

The moment I set up the group, it had the energy of going viral about it and within the first month, 11,000 people had joined. I had tapped into a zeitgeist, a moment in consciousness where many people were learning about the event. Many people joined the group because they had a dream about the event and they put in "The Event" on Facebook and this group came up.

It was like the universe was giving many high vibrational Starseeds information that this event was going to be coming soon and I was the one who was lucky enough to seize the opportunity of that moment; to create a group in order to gather everyone that wanted to learn more about The Event and ultimately to prepare spiritually for this monumental shift in consciousness.

It was an incredible experience creating the Facebook group and we had 22,000 members by the second month and each month it kept on growing exponentially. Everyone who participated said that it was much more than a group. It actually became a spiritual movement.

As the creator of the group, I had a very strict policy of no trolls allowed, no low, negative vibrations allowed. Only exciting, high vibrational posts were permitted.

The policy was that members would be instantly blocked if they were rude or offensive towards anyone else. This was a genius move to make, because it created an incredibly safe container for all of the members to feel like they were held. A place where they could learn to grow and expand in a safe, high vibrational environment.

Very often members would post in the group and we would have 600 to 800 comments. This was a regularity and went on like this for many, many months, with many, many people experiencing full-on spiritual awakenings from being part of the group.

It also helped many people with depression, suicide and mental health problems. Almost every day I would wake up to messages from people who said for the first time in their life, they finally felt like they belonged in a community of people that understood them.

Just receiving one of those messages was enough to satisfy me for my entire life, knowing that I truly am doing God's work, but it bears mentioning that it was absolutely prolific, the number of messages I received from people.

In the creation of this group, it came to my awareness that there were members that were homeless and I thought to myself that it was an absolute no-brainer to utilise the enormous numbers and influence I had on the group to assist our very vulnerable members who were suffering, and did not have the dignity of a place to stay every night.

So, I truly made the most of the large numbers in the group and asked any homeless members to reach out to us, and I created a charity called "Helping One Member at a Time."

To date, we have helped over 40 people. We have raised nearly £100,000 and out of this money, we have been able to give the first month's rent and first month's deposit, which comes to a minimum of £2000 for each person that applied for the fund.

On top of that, they were added to another group, whereby they received all the emotional support they needed as well as friendship. So many amazing things have come out of this charity.

One of the ladies, Tammy, who was the first person that I helped, was a tarot reader who was in her late 50s and was homeless for many, many years, living in her car. When it was brought to the group's attention about Tammy's situation, not only did we raise £2000 for her in 24 hours so that she would no longer be homeless but we also connected her with the members of the group who then reached out to her for tarot card readings. She was then able to set herself up with a good financial income as a result of the support she received from the group.

Tammy is just one example of the amazingness that came out of "The Event Is Happening" group. Suffice to say, it was such an extremely, high vibrational group, that Facebook decided to shadow ban us after the first year so that we no longer appeared in anyone's newsfeed.

CHAPTER FOURTEEN - WHAT HAPPENS IN A TWIN FLAME UNION THAT ASSISTS GAIA TO ASCEND?

I would like to devote the next chapter to speaking about the significance of the solar flash Event and the role of Twin Flames.

As a sacred teacher, or more accurately, a 're-minder,' I've always felt that it is my role to bring together important subject matter such as Twin Flames, Ascension, Enlightened Consciousness and working with the Law of Attraction.

What I have been shown is that Twin Flames are volunteer souls, which means that we have not returned here to re-address karmic imbalances, we came here voluntarily, in order to assist in the great transformation that is currently taking place.

Every 26,000 years, the Earth completes a precession of the equinoxes and transforms its position within the whole solar system in order to come into alignment with Galactic Central. And so, each 26,000 years precipitates the birth of a new Age.

It is my understanding that a clarion call went out to all high-level star beings in the vastest regions of the universe that planet Earth, the solar system and indeed the entire Galaxy were transitioning in vibrational density.

Whenever this great shift happens, Mother Gaia sends out a specific request to Twin Flames to return back to the Earth plane to assist in the great transformation.

There are many reasons why Twin Flames are specifically requested to return back to the earthly plane for this mission. One of them is that Twin Flames who have done the work to come together in physical union have reached a very high level of vibrational balance within their own masculine and feminine energies, within their own selves.

One of the most crucial and deepest medicines that Twin Flames bring is vibrational equilibrium within their own sacred, energetic field.

We must remember that the outer is a reflection of the inner and if Gaia can host a unified Twin Flame pair who has done the spiritual work on themselves to attain equilibrium within their own masculine and feminine energies, then this force field of vibrational equilibrium is sent out into the collective as tones and frequencies, which literally lift Mother Gaia out of the third dimension and place her firmly into the fifth-dimensional frequency band.

The Twin Flames send out vibrationally balanced codes to the electromagnetic field of Gaia, and this is so crucial for Gaia's Ascension because all of the atrocities that have taken place in the last couple of thousand years have sent Mother Earth into a state of deep vibrational imbalance.

Patriarchal energy has completely dominated the magnetic field of Gaia and has brought everyone and everything, including many of the ecosystems of the Earth, into great disarray as a direct result of the imbalance of patriarchy.

This is one of the main reasons why Twin Flames have returned back to the earthly plane to assist in this great planetary Ascension. It is because we are holding the vibration of equilibrium, of balance, between our own masculine and feminine energies.

It is so crucial that Gaia is a host for these Twin Flames that have come into union on the physical plane and that are emanating the frequency of vibrational equilibrium.

Within the universal structure of creation, everything is vibration. Everything in creation is created through the law of vibration. So, if we need to create equilibrium back within Mother Gaia, then vibrational equilibrium is a fundamental necessity for the planet.

In order for that timeline to be accelerated, it is absolutely imperative that as many of Mother-Father God's children as possible have come into, and stabilised in vibrational equilibrium, with their masculine and feminine energies.

Once this occurs, this activates the collapse of the third-dimensional timeline, and enables the fifth-dimensional timeline to entirely come online, due to the fact that one pair of Twins has truly come into vibrational equilibrium.

When a Twin Flame pair has come together again in vibrational equilibrium, this could be likened to a tuning fork. When this sacred union occurs, the soul unit sends out a tone to all that is, which informs the whole, that one pair has truly arrived home at the place of vibrational equilibrium.

I use the analogy of a tuning fork, as it is a wonderful way of explaining how vibrations work. As soon as one person attains and stabilises in a masterful vibration, this then automatically affects everybody who is blessed to come into contact with that person. For example, if you get a tuning fork and you put it in a room with many other tuning forks, they all start attuning to the same higher frequency.

One of the main reasons the planet is in the state that it is in is because we have collectively gone out of balance. And so, in order for the planet to ascend, it has to come back into balance. And we as children of God have to come into balance with our masculine and feminine energies within.

It is this which will bring all the ecosystems such as the oceans, the forests, and all the aspects of creation back into balance, harmony and equilibrium.

This is one of the main fundamental reasons why Mother-Father God has decreed it necessary for Twin Flames to return back to the Earth plane at this particular point on the evolutionary cycle, and this is because the Twins emanate the tone of balance and equilibrium within their psychic fields that Gaia may efficiently find her own balance and her own equilibrium once again. As it is within so it is without.

This is an extremely important reason why Twin Flames received the Clarion Call from the universe to reunite again back on the earthly plane, at the time of this great shift, this great planetary Awakening, that we are all experiencing.

The other main reason is because the energy that is experienced when Twins reunite after a period of separation - the bliss and rapture that is activated within the heart consciousness of the Twins, each time they come back into physical union - is of such a potently high vibration that it is literally this, which will lift the planet out of the third dimension and restore it back safely into the fifth-dimensional, heaven consciousness reality.

I hope that you are able to ascertain the potency of what I am sharing with you. There is nothing more powerful energetically on this Earth than Twins reuniting after a period of separation.

When a true genuine bona fide Twin Flame pair comes into recognition of each other, this then activates the codes of unconditional love, which, when released, opens the golden gate to the Zero-point field.

As one enters through the Zero-point field of consciousness, this is when one truly awakens to one's full and complete multiple-dimensionality, as prior to this entry point and ensuing stabilisation in fifth-dimensional consciousness, one realises that one has just been very much hovering in the lower fourth-dimensional realms, which like the third dimension, are riddled with duality.

Through the experience of Unconditional Love and the entering of the heart portal, finally, the soul returns home to the place of eternal, perpetual and abiding union with self and God.

As has been mentioned many times in this book, the fifth dimension is the Zero-point field, the gateway point to all multiple-dimensional realms of consciousness. The fifth dimension is pure love, pure sacred marriage, pure union, pure celebration, ecstasy, rapture, bliss and so much more…

Twin Flames hold the trump vibration and therefore are able to eradicate lower timelines and templates through their unified field. This is one of the main reasons why Mother-Father God has decreed the return of the 144,000 original Twin Flames that fractalled off at the moment of creation.

CHAPTER FIFTEEN - CHILDREN OF TWIN FLAMES

Next, I would like to speak about a topic which is extremely close to many of our hearts and that is the subject of the children who have incarnated with either parents or step-parents who are Twin Flames... I would like to share in some detail what I have been shown about their specific and unique role in this current planetary Ascension.

Here I am referring to the children that are born into Twin Flame unions, as well as the children who are born with a parent who is a Twin Flame and is set to unite with their Twin Flame on the physical earthly level.

Many of these children are carrying the living template of the unified Twin Flame field. These souls will be activated with their own spiritual awakening at perfect timeline moments, in order to align their physical bodies with the incoming light that these unions bring.

In these recent Ascension energies, many of these highly sensitive children have been clearing vast amounts of personal planetary and collective residues in order to stand as clear channels to receive the Ascension codes, as they are being fully activated within the Earth matrix.

These recent Ascension frequencies have had a huge effect on everyone and the children that are involved energetically with bona fide Twins Flames will have been feeling these energetics extremely intensely.

Most children that are connected to Twin Flames are extremely highly evolved, galactic beings who have incarnated at this time to, in most cases, also establish a successful Twin Flame relationship on the earthly plane. They have also incarnated with extraordinary gifts that will assist in this great Awakening that we are all experiencing.

These children are highly evolved souls and are extraordinarily intelligent, compassionate and empathic. Many of them are connected to the dolphin and whale family and as such, are bringing forth an unprecedented level of emotional sophistication and wisdom.

Many of the souls who have come through a parent who is a Twin Flame have contracted with the parent's true Twin Flame to have an extremely deep soul connection and love in this lifetime. Indeed, many of you will find that your Twin Flame is the true energetic soul parent of your child and the biological parent in many ways was the provider of the seed.

This relationship, that is about to show up in the lives of many Twin Flames and the children related to these unions, is one of the most exquisite to behold. And from the higher perspective it has been observed that many of you are seen crying out for these children to come back into your life.

Dearest beloveds, all is unfolding with meticulous precision regarding each of your unique, earthly reunions with your Twin Flame. Rest assured that all of the clearing and symptoms that go along with this sacred union are serving a most grand purpose at this auspicious time of critical mass of Twin Flame union.

The children that are connected to bona fide Twin souls are extremely high vibrating beings on the whole and are masterful in the realms of empathy and intuition. Many of them display highly charismatic and mystical qualities too. They have been hardwired in their DNA to be part of this great, grand holy reunion template that is subsuming Terra Gaia now.

These children carry the templates to be able to hold the high quota of crystalline energy that is born from the energetics that are released from this reunion. And so, it is no surprise that they have been experiencing huge energetic shifts recently.

Watch over these precious beings at this time and remember they are extremely sensitive and receptive to any sort of vibrational healing modalities, such as flower essences and homeopathy. They are also extremely receptive to colour and sound therapy and visualisation of any sort. Keep these ones shielded and protected by calling upon Archangel Michael to lovingly give them their blue cloaks that shield their energy fields and teach them to ask Archangel Michael for protection themselves.

Indeed, these are a profoundly precious and highly sensitive group of beings that have signed up to be part of the most spectacular love story the Earth has ever known.

These souls are destined to do huge things in the world in the years to come and their number one purpose for coming to this world has always been to shine.

The Magic of this Book That You are Holding

I would like to share with you all now an amazing synchronicity that I have experienced while writing this book. It has been such a joyful, healing and comforting experience; sharing all of these sacred words with you all and having this experience of journeying with the spirit of this book. A book that has been waiting for God knows how many lifetimes to be written! And so, as I align with the creation of this book and meet and dance with the spirit of this book, it is indeed a most wondrous experience.

Within the first couple of weeks of writing this book and getting these words down on sacred paper, I had the most magical experience.

I had a knowing deep inside of me that this book would not reach the masses in what you would term a third-dimensional way. Throughout the entire process of birthing this creation, I have been clearly shown that this book would be born and exist within the fifth-dimensional realm of consciousness, which means it is a living entity that exists within the heart of every being alive.

I was shown by my spirit team that this book will be read by millions of people in the world and this would occur through all of us who read the book, passing it along and buying this book for our nearest and dearest, soul family members.

As we pass on these sacred words, a huge door will open up for us - myself included - who are basking in the glory of this very long awaited message.

Back to the synchronicity. I had a very clear vision that this is how this book will reach the mass consciousness, through word-of-mouth and through being passed hand to hand. I received a very clear vision of Elizabeth Gilbert's book “Eat, Pray, Love” and I remembered that that was the exact promise of her book, that everyone would read it and then pass it onto the people that they love. And indeed, that is how I came across and read that wonderful book, which I read maybe two or three times and finally got me to travel to Bali.

That book came into my consciousness and I thought, if Elizabeth can do it, we can do it!

Within less than 24 hours, my beautiful soul sister invited me to a sauna deep in the woods in England where I live, bearing in mind, I moved into this property on the 9th of November 2020 and I started writing this book on the 11th of the 11th.

I have been told by my spirit team that this book will be finished (and I'm getting goosebumps as I write this) not released - but in my hands, by the 21st December 2020.

Back to the synchronicity. I remembered Elizabeth Gilbert and her message to us all and this inspired me to create a powerful intention to the universe that I would use the same method Elizabeth Gilbert used, which was to encourage all the readers to share this book by passing it on from hand to hand and mouth to mouth.

Within 24 hours of receiving this clear message from my spirit team, I was led to this sauna in the UK. Everyone in this sauna was naked and really enjoying the heat, being far in the depths of the forest in a lovely, warm sauna but there was one lady fully dressed, wearing walking boots, sitting by the fire and there she was reading the book, "Eat, Pray, Love."

I was blown away because I thought to myself, "That is what you call a sign from the universe," and it was glaringly obvious to me at that moment that truly this book that you are holding in your hands has a spirit. And it has a spirit that is meant to be passed along to as many Brothers and Sisters as we can possibly reach.

This book is a dot connector of the highest order, that will explain so much and clarify so much for so many, helping so many of us to access higher dimensional levels of consciousness, through marrying and merging the left and the right brain and truly understanding from a divine, angelic perspective what is going on.

Bearing in mind, this is my own personal perspective and this is a reminder to only ever take what resonates with you and disregard the rest. I am sharing my own personal experience of what I would call overdosing with God - but that is probably another book entirely…

It bears mentioning that when I had my spiritual awakening when I was 21, chanting the mantra *Om Namah Shivaya* on top of the Himalayan mountain, I had the experience where, after chanting the mantra what felt like at least 30,000 times in one day, I looked above me and I saw a flash of light. I knew in that moment that I was in the presence of God. I knew it was God because I had rejected the word God due to my Catholic programming.

But in that moment, I remembered that God is love and love is eternal truth and God is truth and God is forever. And God is the creator and God is my creator. And my soul was born in God. My soul was born in eternal love. My soul shall return to eternal love.

I will definitely be speaking a lot more about this in my upcoming book, "The Autobiography of my Spiritual Awakening."

The message of this whole entire chapter is to please share this book openly and lovingly from your heart with those that you most love and most cherish so that they may get to have the experience of so many important dots being put together.

Of course, these words are only meant for those who resonate with them and your heart will guide you perfectly who to share these sacred words with.

So, thank you all so much for being part of this journey of getting this message out far and wide to all of our Brothers and Sisters, so that we remember that divine love is our birthright, that we have all signed up for it, that we live in a great and benevolent universe and Mother-Father God is great and wonderful.

May we all remember we are all precious children. And this universe, this sacred Earth, has been created for all of us as a playground for our spirits, for our divine eternal selves, to play in and bask in the presence and remembrance of our true divinity.

Lately I have been very much tuning into the deep knowing that this earthly experience is the final culmination of God experiencing itself in physicality. And therefore, it could be argued that humans and all earthly beings are the closest molecular structure there is to divinity in the universe.

Maybe this is why they say that the angels are jealous of our human bodies.

CHAPTER SIXTEEN - WINTER SOLSTICE 2020

As I've mentioned, I was inspired to birth this book from the 11:11 portal to the 21st of December portal 2020. My spirit team were very adamant that the winter solstice point of 2020 would be an extremely significant Ascension marker in the Collective.

I would now like to speak now about what I have been shown about the energies of the 21st of December.

With this particular planetary alignment, I am being shown that energetically a cosmic map is being created, which aligns perfectly with galactic central. What this means is that, on the higher dimensional levels of consciousness, a pattern or a map is being formed astrologically and astronomically, which is in effect creating a star gate or a portal to Galactic Central. As I've spoken about in my energy reports since they first began in May 2015, Galactic Central holds within its central core, photonic light particles.

Photonic Light Particles

Photonic light particles are also known as God particles.

As we align with this particular astrological portal date, we will be, in effect, creating an etheric pathway to the stars, an etheric pathway connecting the portal of the Earth plane, deeply in alignment with Galactic Central.

This means that all of the photonic light particles that are continuously spewing forth from Galactic Central will be reaching the Earth realm unencumbered.

The triumphant success of this work is also connected to the huge amount of shadow work that humanity has cleared in the last year. That has resulted in the collective bearing witness to an en masse collective spiritual awakening.

Many, many Brothers and Sisters have awoken after being fully entrenched and identified in the third-dimensional matrix programme, to the realization that there is much more to this reality than what we have been indoctrinated to believe.

It is very important to know that one person coming into awakened consciousness is all powerful, as we are all micros of the macro. And due to the year 2020, we have witnessed an absolutely unprecedented amount of humanity awakening spiritually.

As I mentioned earlier, we are all micros of the macro. And so, when one consciousness ascends out of the false matrix of the third dimension and comes home to the higher dimensional realms of consciousness, this automatically lifts the vibration of the whole entire planet.

And that is what has been going on en masse, with so many people being spiritually awakened and freeing themselves of the third-dimensional, prison matrix consciousness.

This in and of itself is directly lifting the planet's vibration and as the planet's vibration is being lifted, it is aligning on an energetic level with Galactic Central.

As this occurs, this ensures that the influx of photonic light particles, or God particles, reaches humanity with great ease and swiftness.

Also, with regards to the photonic light particles that spewed forth from Galactic Central for the grand conjunction of the 21st of December 2020, I have been shown that The Earth's collective is about to receive a brand new geometrical patterning of photonic light particles that are connected to the higher strands of our DNA, i.e., these photonic light particles will be communicating directly with our so-called previous junk DNA, which has now been brought back online. These photonic light particles will be interlinking with the previously perceived junk DNA in order to assist humanity to truly become one on an individual level with one's higher self.

On that day, the 21st of December 2020, I hosted a large global meditation with over 800 people in this meditation. We were guided to work with the Guardian Aboriginal elders at Uluru who requested that as many as possible of God's children all come together in our global Ascension groups to assist in the opening of the Magic Box.

It was revealed to me that the Magic Box was seeded by the Pleiadian beings at the time of Lemuria, when Lemuria was a Pleiadian colony and Uluru was the birthplace of this civilisation.

Uluru is the umbilical cord point that connects the Earth to the heart of Mother Gaia/Father Sky. I was shown that the magic box would be opened if humanity reached a particular level of consciousness whereby enough of the Brothers and Sisters had woken up.

Indeed, I was shown that the opening of the Magic Box was intricately connected to a critical mass point being reached.

This Magic Box contains the energy of the mythical beings who have been guarding Earth in the lower-dimensional or one could say fourth-dimensional realms of consciousness.

Here I am referring to the Dragons, the Fairies and indeed all mythical and mystical creatures.

It is the vibration of the elemental beings of nature that has been kept safely in the Magic Box awaiting the time that humanity is able to coexist in a world whereby these mythical beings are honoured, acknowledged and respected.

CHAPTER SEVENTEEN - YESHUA AND MAGDALENE

This book would not be complete if I did not share with you the incredible information that my spirit team shared with me about the sacred union of Yeshua and Magdalene. As I mentioned before and will explain in much greater detail in my upcoming autobiography of my spiritual awakening, when I experienced my first Kundalini awakening, age 21, on top of the Himalayan mountain; the day after I had that experience, I looked into my brother's eyes and I could see clearer than day the Christ-Self that had eternally dwelled in him. I could see it clearer than the blue sky above me. I recognized the divine Christ-Self that he is.

The fact that I recognized him to be the Christ made me automatically realise that I too must also carry the Flame of the feminine Christ within me. And in the moment of that realisation, I realised that every single being alive carries the frequency and the Flame of Christ within them. This was such an enormous revelation for me, as I was so shocked that this was not taught or reminded to us from any aspects of our society.

As soon as I saw him and recognized the Christ-Self in him, in me and in everyone, I then started to receive many, many downloads about the lifetime and indeed timeline of Yeshua and Magdalene.

I'm not exactly sure what happened to my consciousness, but it was like a door opened and suddenly I was shown the timeline of what happened between Yeshua and Magdalene. I will now share with you all that I was shown.

I was shown that Mary Magdalene was born into a family of high priestesses and much like the Dalai Lama's role, she was recognized as being a very high-level spiritual avatar from the moment of her birth.

I was shown that she grew up in the temples of Isis and she was surrounded by wise and mystical women and was exposed to the ways of the Holy Grail, also known as sacred sexuality and sacred alchemy.

I was shown that she grew up in the temples of Isis, receiving very, very high-level training and initiations as a tantric priestess.

I was shown that she met Yeshua around the age of 18 and she was fully enlightened when they met. And through her enlightenment, she recognized him as her divine beloved. It was literally through her eyes, through her own perception, which ignited the seed of Christ in him to become the fruit or the Flame of the Christic being. It was through her perception and recognition of the true identity of her beloved which activated the Christ seal within him to fully activate, which triggered his own enlightenment.

I was shown that she was always considered to be more spiritually advanced than Yeshua and it was widely understood that the role of the divine feminine was to be the teacher and spiritual protector of the divine masculine. And the role of the divine masculine was to be the earthly protector of the divine feminine.

I was shown that as soon as Yeshua became illuminated, this was a very powerful experience for the Earth and for the collective, because a man who is fully enlightened serves to truly ground and anchor the highest spiritual codes into the earthly grid, whereas a woman in a state of absolute enlightenment is although extremely powerful on all levels, her consciousness is deeply connected to the unseen realms and to the higher dimensional planes of consciousness. And therefore, a woman's enlightenment is very much connected to full and extended mastery in the unseen realms, whereas when a divine masculine becomes enlightened, this is always extremely powerful for the earthly plane.

Through Yeshua's enlightenment, I was shown that he attracted many followers and they moved around Israel and the Middle East, teaching the way of sacred divine union, Twin soul partnership and the true meaning of the Holy Grail. I was shown that the main reason why Yeshua and Magdalene returned back to the earthly plane was to restore the Holy Grail back to humanity.

The Holy Grail refers to the alchemical process that happens when you transform the lead of the third-dimensional consciousness to the gold of the Christed higher self.

This alchemy is very often triggered by the recognition of the true divine consort on the inner and outer planes of consciousness.

As I have mentioned many times in this book, as soon as the true identity of the Divine consort/Twin soul is revealed, this activates hitherto dormant codes, particularly in the pituitary and the pineal gland.

Once these secretions are unified and released, this activates the transformation of the vessel from carbon to crystalline and this is what the Holy Grail is referencing.

The Holy Grail is also very much connected to the sacred womb of the divine feminine and one can only truly access the vibratory frequencies of the Holy Grail through the portal of the divine, awakened feminine.

Mary Magdalene is a perfect example of one who carries the codes of the Holy Grail, as she is a true living embodiment of Enlightenment and has transformed her consciousness from the lead of the ego to the gold of the Christed Self.

One of the most important reasons why Yeshua and Magdalene returned back to the Earth plane was to restore the Twin soul partnership template back into humanity's consciousness. It was widely known 2000 years ago by the Essenes and all who followed Yeshua and Magdalene that the greatest vibratory medicine for planet Earth is activated when true divine partners come into recognition and sacred reunion with each other. As this momentum is so extraordinarily powerful - spiritually and physically - it literally lifts the third dimension out of its somewhat quarantined, matrix vibration into the high, exalted, rapturous vibrations that can be referred to as Heaven on Earth.

It was widely known that true love was the most powerful force in the universe and therefore Yeshua and Magdalene's mission was to be living examples of this true Twin soul template.

The purpose was to teach about the ways of divine partnership and also to inspire divine partnership in all those that came into contact with them. It is widely known that Yeshua and Magdalene travelled around the world on their mission and there are certain areas in southern France known as The Cathar regions, whereby it is believed that Magdalene spent a great deal of her time.

This is indeed true according to my spiritual guides and I was shown that her mission to Europe was in order to share the Teachings of the Holy Grail.

One of the most important aspects of the Legacy and mission of Christ and Magdalene was to remind the Earth and all her children that Unconditional Love reigns supreme in the universe. That Unconditional Love is the force that creates every blade of grass and every grain of sand. Unconditional Love is the force that turns a seed into a flower and turns a sperm and an egg into a divine soul.

Unconditional Love is the most important energy in the universal matrix and our job as humans is to return home to the heart consciousness which reigns supreme on a spiritual level - that we may become one with our God creator self, who resides eternally in our own consciousness.

Mary Magdalene was well aware of the Earth grids seeing as she was a truly enlightened soul and she knew that the Twin Flame Union was going to be the master template for the Earth and would ensure the Earth being fully released from its third-dimensional quarantine state.

She was a grid worker of the highest order, working very deeply with the pyramids of Egypt, as well as the sacred sites in France and England.

I will share with you all in greater detail about what I was shown about the relationship between Yeshua and Magdalene in my upcoming autobiography of my spiritual Awakening but I will close this chapter with a channelled message that I received about the seed of the Christ-Self that dwells in all.

The Seed of Christ

The seed of Christ lays within each and every one of us. The seed of Christ is our original divine blueprint. There is only one self, one universal Christ and we are all equally loved and valued aspects of this prism of crystallised diamond consciousness.

Once the seed of Christ consciousness has been nourished and tended and begins to be revealed from outside in, a huge transformation then takes over our being as the DNA is flooded with these solar codes that activate and enliven the seed of Christ within us to blossom into its full potential.

It is in the sacred sphere of Christ consciousness, that the union with the beloved forever is. This is the frequency where the sacred marriage is enacted and celebrated in every moment.

Christ consciousness is the space of home.

FINAL WORDS

We have so much to look forward to, so much growth, so much expansion, so much opening to the light beautiful divine Brothers and Sisters.

My prayer is that everyone reading these words truly arrives home at the Zero-point field of consciousness; the present moment where all timelines converge and your soul truly knows on every level of your being, that it has arrived home.

That is my blessing for all of us. May we all bask in the glory of our divinity, in remembrance that the present moment is the greatest gift our creator has given us.

May you drop into presence, may you share your divine presence with your family, may you be present with everyone - be that the lady in the post office, the man in the garage or your elderly father - may we offer each other our presence.

We are all so worthy of that. We are so worthy to be honoured, to be cherished, to be loved.

I love you all.

Now would be a perfect moment to relax as consciousness for a short moment.

EPILOGUE

This great, grand love that you know exists deep in your soul is real, is so very, very real and was placed in your sacred heart by your creator self to be activated and awoken in the moment of preordained divine timing.

Within all of you in the vast storehouse of your earthly bodies lie gateways and portals and indeed stations that have hitherto laid dormant, awaiting the moment of divine recognition of the true sacred beloved of the soul.

Once this actual deep soul recognition has taken place, the initiate experiences this as a visionary and heart-based merge with the true divine consort. This serves to unlock each of the gateways in the pineal centre, which then releases the sacred knowledge of one's true multi-dimensional nature.

This is felt predominantly in the heart centre, as the energetic keys that the beloved possesses unlock the vast fields of soul knowing within that love is the only true reality that exists and is real.

This also activates the knowing that time exists only in the present moment. which brings forth mastery over timeline management and realignment and unlocks in the heart centre, a deep emotional alignment with the original soul, blueprint matrix.

This is a time for all of you now to bathe in the most exquisite love from your higher creator self.

When one has come into true recognition of the Twin Flame and experienced the ensuing expanded consciousness that comes along with that; in that moment there is a glimpse and a comprehension of quite how far down the rabbit hole this Twin Flame connection truly goes.

The initiate experiences breakthrough after breakthrough and healing after healing, with an ever breath-taking alignment with the radiance of the higher Christed self.

When God sends the one whose keys fit your locks, all will see this in the joy and light that emanates from the core of your solar earthly matrix. This is one who has awakened and is fully stabilised and aligned in God consciousness, radiating the mastery codes of Twin Flame union.

TWIN FLAMES AND THE EVENT - MORE BOOK TESTIMONIES

I didn't think I would add this section to this book, but I followed the advice of many self-publishers who recommended getting a street team to read part of the manuscript prior to its release date in order to leave a review on the day of its release.

I gathered my team together and nothing on God's great Earth could prepare me for the response that came back within hours of me sending out the manuscript.

Every single person reported identical experiences, intense emotions, crying, goosebumps, shivering, past life memories coming back, lucid dreams, and out-of-body experiences.

Literally every single person was reporting extraordinary feedback from reading the book. So my publishing team and I decided that we would devote a part of the book to sharing some of the incredible testimonies that I received a few days before this book's publication..

So I share these sacred words, with heartfelt gratitude, to all of the brothers and sisters who stepped forward to a be part of this important team.

This first review is from my soul sister Christine.

Thank you
For coming so natural magically in my life
The Event is Happening group
Long time seemed to be, my window to the world
In a time
When everything felt lost
It kept me alive, through days and nights
Of solitude, despair, trauma.
It just helped me
To continue, to understand, to heal.
To become aware,
To connect to my heart,
And feel connected
Again.
It is amazing
What you have created.
Biblical and epic.
So many people and beings
All over the world and the cosmos
Coming together,
Like friends,
Brothers and sisters,
Family
Joining to become
As One
In the Love
In the Light
In the Glory
Of God
Wow
Like living the dream

And now your book
What a treasure
So
I would say
PEOPLE READ
JEN MCCARTY´S
TWIN FLAMES & THE EVENT
book
DIVE IN DEEP
COME OUT
WITH YOUR HEART
AND WINGS
WIDE OPEN.
TO EMBRACE
THE LOVE OF YOUR LIFE,
AND BE EMBRACED
BY ALL THAT IS.
IT IS A SUPERNATURAL
HOMECOMING
FINALLY.
Every word written is so intimate
It works on a variety of levels
on the inside
on the outside
It is pure.
It is true.
Everything experienced and shared
Through it
Is just so trustworthy and holy
Have read these first chapters
In several parts

Witnessing and enjoying the journey
It sends me within myself.
With all the ahas, and wows, and ahas and Ohs
And tears and joy
Seems like puzzling together,
Connecting all these dots.
From the very beginning of existence
Mine and the collective.
Most beautiful feeling
Of being overwhelmed.
So so grateful
Every encounter with the world outside,
People, animals, nature, unseen realms
Becomes just marvelous
Feels real
HEAVEN ON EARTH
So
This book is
UNIQUELY FIRST CLASS
It just works
Transforming, healing, alchemical,
Uniting, enchanting, adorable
Initiating the wonder of
A divine love story
We all came for
We all are prepared for
This Earth and universe
Is there for
So again
DANKE JEN
It was and is such a great honor

Reading this uplifting beginning
Of your first book
Like merging in an everlasting bliss
To be also a part of your life
With all this sacred waves and ways
Witnessing your devoted work for God
And us
So tireless and courageous
Is a gift
Happy and honored to continue
This will be
AN INTERNATIONAL
BESTSELLER
because it is worthy of it.
It just works.
Opening doors and portals
In body mind spirit and cosmos
We waited for.

From the German poet
Friedrich Schiller
To you
Jen McCarty

~ Dignity of Women
Honor the women! They're roses celestial
Twining and weaving in lives terrestrial,
Weaving the bond of the most blessed love,
Veiled in the Graces' most modest attire
Nourish they watchful the e'erlasting fire
Of lovely feelings with hand from above ~

You remind us
How blessed we are
Thank you
Christine

Jen,

Just finished reading this first draft of the first chapters of this book. Fantastic. Not only is it fantastic, I personally had Heart, Root, sacral, solar plexus and Kundalini activations up my spine the whole time I was reading it. Can't wait for the next installment Much Love
Debbie O'Connor

Hello Jen,

I am struggling to put my feelings into words because reading this manuscript was such a powerful and activating experience for me. I felt goosebumps running up my spine and I resonated deeply with everything in it.

The three words that can best describe the impact of your book are remembering, sovereignty, Love. This is such an activating thought to remember that we were chosen among many souls wanting to incarnate on Earth at this powerful time.

To me, this book is a very adequate tool to help us navigate the current reality and its challenges with the two-world split between 3D and 5D. We are showing up every day to be in service for humanity and help the collective shift towards 5D. This is an arduous but so beautiful. Our role is to anchor the higher frequencies on Earth by radiating our own Lovelight in the Universe.

On a personal level, this book is so empowering because it leads to unconditional self-love. It reminded me so beautifully that Love is not to be found in the external but inside of us.

The explanation of the different types of relationships was illuminating for me. It clarifies so many doubts and fears, it really helped me understand why some things occurred this way in my life. I understood a lot better the nature of the interactions between the Masculine and Feminine, within us and in the external.

I am really looking forward to reading the whole book and the workbook going alongside it. Thank you for the beautiful work you are doing for humanity, I am truly humbled to walk this Ascension path by your side. Much love,

Elodie

Already upon having read the first chapters of your amazing book, I feel full of gratitude for being led to this journey of connecting with my twin flame.

Your book is written in a language, which is accessible to most people, and yet very deep and profound. The whole text shows that you have deep knowledge and connection to the core of all wisdom. I do not remember having seen this deep knowledge about twin flames in any other book before.

It is my honest opinion that your book will be used as a guidance for people, either searching for their twin flame or realizing which kind of relationship they are in/have been in. Some might even be encouraged to consider whether they should stay in their relationship or not.

Also your chapter about your own ascension journey gives the reader a lot of useful and beautiful insight. Others will be likely to follow the same way into enlightenment - reaching the Zero-point consciousness.

I look forward to reading the rest of the book and highly recommend others to read these wise words by Jen McCarty, which are so full of life, love, and light.

Thank you and namaste.

Esther Oekaer, Denmark

When I started reading the book, I felt a pleasant nervousness inside me. Like some deja vu, it feels like I read it all a long time ago or knew it from before.

My life never went in the direction it went to my close friends and acquaintances and no matter how much I wanted to have a quiet, ordinary and seemingly normal life, it always drove me out of my comfort zone into some situations and areas I was unwilling to follow and accept. In the end I would never have another option but to accept life as it was given to me.

From my childhood , I felt different from most children and it was as if I always had a higher path. From a young age, I was interested in the higher meaning and aspects of life, so as a child I wanted to learn on my own initiative what God is and after school I hung out with a girl who was baptized, which I am not and my parents are not believers, so I would teach various prayers at home, one that stuck in my memory was a prayer for the protection of my family and I would pray it every night.

Like I said, my life from a young age was different from other children and in many ways more challenging and difficult because I didn't have the firm support and support of my family in that some deeper, spiritual and even loving aspect. My sister often abused me both physically and mentally, and my parents had an unstable relationship and often quarreled.

From a young age, therefore, I felt a deep urge to know God and discover the true meaning of love.

I have been dreaming since the age of twelve about true and reciprocated romantic love on all levels.

This book only gave me confirmation that I am really on the right path and that no matter how difficult it is to progress in a spiritual sense, because there are a lot of detours and wrong directions, I feel that I have come a long way. My inner critic constantly makes me doubt my achievement, but the messages that confirm that I have really progressed appear more and more to me in synchronicities.

Although I am aware that I still have a lot of work to do, and I am not mistaken at all, this book is another subtle but strong confirmation that I am in the right place and on the right path.

I came across the concept of twin flame a couple of years ago and my inner critic didn't even let me think I could have my own twin flame after reading that it happens in the last incarnation on Earth. At the time, I didn't even dream that this Great Awakening could happen and that I would realize I was Starseed.

I am very excited about all this and again I have hope that I will really meet my twin flame or that there is a great opportunity for that.

Reading your book, I realized that everything that my soul constantly whispers to me still makes sense.

Although I have not had my Kundalini awakening, I look forward to all that lies ahead of me on the spiritual path and I am grateful to you from the bottom of my heart that this book has reached my hands and prepares me for my very possible reunion with my twin flame half.

I've had a lot of disappointments in relationships in my life because my standards have always been pretty high even though sometimes out of misconception I agreed to less just that I have a relationship too, but now I know why I'm alone.

With special thanks to you, for explaining to me so beautifully, simply and yet so powerfully the dynamics of the union of twin souls in this wonderful moment in our existence.

I am grateful to you forever!

Marija

Thank you for blessing me with the opportunity to read this most powerful manuscript, which I received on this auspicious day of 2:2. Just by reading your e-mail, with the attachment of the book, triggered my Kundalini. I instantly felt this heat energy, like a burning flame, in my lower back.

This book is so well written, and there is fluidity and sequence within the chapters. I was so magnetised by this book that I read it in a few hours.

The first line of the prologue intensified the burning sensation at the base of my spine. It sets the scene clearly, so that the brothers and sisters who are unfamiliar with the twin flame journey, will have a sudden innerstanding of this process.

As soon as I hit the first chapter, I experienced a tingling sensation all along my spinal column, which then settled as a ball of energy between my shoulder blades.

I resonated with your simple yet powerful explanation of the concept of 144 souls. For me, this was confirmation that I was part of the Starseed community. It cleared so many doubts and lack of knowledge around the TF energy and shed light on the different types of relationships.

As I read through, I started feeling very cold and experienced a roller coaster of emotions...that of joy, fulfillment, union with my twin. I felt this ball of energy and tightness around my throat chakra. When I saw the word 'Merkabah' I had goosebumps all over.

When you explained about the zero-point field, I had this sense of homecoming, I was there; I can finally rest and be at peace with myself. I also felt this massive shift in energy, I felt grounded. I even had a synchronicity with linear time e.g 14:40, 14:41 and 14:44.

Thank you once again Jen for this amazing opportunity and I can't wait to read the rest of this beautiful piece of divine work.

Much love,

Gaitree

What a wonderful start to this amazing coming book. I absolutely love the conversation with God that Jen had before starting this journey, which is so deep and profound.

It is all about looking within and find unconditional love within ourselves, rather than looking for it outside of ourselves. I deeply resonated with this.

We, as Starseeds, Lightworkers, Warriors of Light, are here to serve humanity and so need to learn how to operate from the heart centre in all that we do.

This book clearly shows us the way to do this. It activates something within us that pushes us to look much much deeper within.

Losing her platform comprising 150,000 followers was so tough but how wonderful to see that a book came out of it? This is how the Universe works.

When one door closes, another opens.

I have learned so much about divine partnerships too. The way Jen describes Twin Flames is ever so profound that it gives me tingles all over.

It has been the same thing while reading about the Divine Feminine and the book of Gnosis. In fact, I would say that I have felt electricity all throughout my body while reading this.

I have never heard of Catalyst Twins before and I felt incredible goosebumps when I read about that. I have been seeing 144 a huge amount of times and these synchronicities makes sense to me now.

I can see how this book will activate millions of people's DNA and I cannot wait to read the next chapters!

Thank you so much Jen for all that you do for humanity. You do this with such passion and open heart.

You are deeply loved and appreciated

~Aditi~

AFTERWORD - WRITTEN BY LAURA EISENHOWER

Twin Flame union and how we are magnetized by nature to returning to that within and with another is the driving force behind Spiritual evolution as humans. It is what gives us passion, motivation and inspiration. It is that inner longing that puts us on a quest, first starting with getting to know who we truly are and what it means to be our full authentic divine self.

Human consciousness in full alignment with the creative imagination, the Zero-point unified field, and the anchoring of the Mother energies back into the Earth body are how we can begin to rebuild the Tree of Life, out of the duality we have existed in.

We move through many stages in life in order to embody this internal architecture. Going through the Dark night of the Soul, wandering through the Underworlds and experiencing different aspects of ourselves, means we can begin to integrate Archetypes and achieve wholeness.

When the ego is willing to let go and surrender to this greater experience, it brings us closer to Divine Union and our Twin flame. We have to constantly release what doesn't serve us and rescue our mental bodies from what keeps us locked into an artificial inverted and reversal system, which keeps us stuck in a time loop.

Many don't realize that in order to break this loop, we need to see what attachments we have and step outside of the world of appearances and projection, to find our true self again.

Once we find our truth frequency, the body begins to respond, transform and heal and a greater priority and focus begins to take center stage in our lives. The power of synchronicities gets stronger as we live in a more soul-centered way and so greater meaning is found in every connection we make and Soul mates find their way to us, which continues taking us into a greater unfoldment towards the Twin flame union.

The Mother energies are coming in so strongly in this Stellar Activation cycle Ascension window, which is the end of a 26,000 year cycle. This connects us with powerful transmissions that help us to see the health of our full self and energetic body, and begins the deep healing process and rediscovery of the greater Love story that we are all a part of.

Expanding our consciousness into other dimensions and grounding with the Earth helps us to turn on dormant DNA, which brings us closer to heirogamic union which is encoded in the higher strands of our DNA.

This is how we access other Harmonic Universes and begin to move from carbon-based beings to Crystalline. The energetic circulation that comes from being conscious helps to clear out programs, it purifies our Chakra system and we begin to experience the true love story of Creation.

Releasing ourselves from the Archonic Matrix is similar to going through a break-up. It is a relationship that we have had for some time and some have grown so accustomed to it, that many often aren't able to see a much vaster and more divine reality.

The patriarchal programming that reveals itself in the Saturn-Moon matrix is how we can begin to understand why our DNA has unavailable strands known as Junk

DNA. In actual fact this this so-called Junk is a treasure to discover and in doing the inner work and embarking on a path of self-discovery and connecting closely with Earth, Spirit and Cosmos, we can begin to see ourselves emerging out of the false Matrix of manipulation and control to embrace our True love destiny. The Christ-Sophia Divine template that dwells within.

The poisoning of Earth elements, false power structures and the media manipulations have made it very challenging to stand in our power and so we are injured, wounded, traumatized and dealing with the heaviness of so much toxicity. Much of the trauma from previous lifetimes is unconscious and so trigger events and psychological operations continually throw us off and into fear, without fully realizing the larger picture of what they are attempting to sabotage.

We interpret it as reality or the human condition, when in actual fact it's an artificially induced problem, reaction, solution scenario, that only disempowers us. It is easy to control a humanity who holds so much unconsciousness and so starting from childhood, the indoctrination begins.

Social engineering, Mockingbird media (distorted information and narratives covering up Deep-state activities) and the very fabric of our culture and society holds these detrimental distortions that keep us in a state of dis-harmony and sub-personalities that aren't an authentic representation of our inner divine masculine and feminine.

Ultimately, the battle is won within, and we have to take the steps necessary to claim victory and our full sovereignty, by consciously removing ourselves from these harmful false programs that keep us in a constant patterning of broken and unfulfilling relationships.

Disease is very rooted in this, because the body has a hard time adjusting to something that is false, superficial or in reversal coding. It can be very difficult at times to break free from, because all this really targets our self-esteem and sense of self worth, as we are rewarded more for going along with the set stereotypes and acclimating to them.

Our true nature and expression for many got belittled and mistreated early on and later in life when there is an attempt to create a pure, soulful and meaningful Sacred Union relationships, it often leads to a broken heart and much confusion. If one's partner isn't the right match and it's only based on physical attraction or chemistry, it gets very risky, but there are many important Soul partners that play an important role in our own self-discovery and ability to consciously heal from ancestral patterns and societal conditioning of what roles we should play as genders. When we work on purifying our negative Ego and inner elements, the Earth responds.

It is our willingness to end harmful agreements, step into our divine center and embrace the true love story that allows for us to embody the happily ever after. No one can really complete us, but they can share in that divine spark as two emerging from the one. This is the ultimate destiny for all of us and in the process of getting there, we help humanity wake up and align with organic Ascension that takes us to higher Earth energies.

Since the Sumerian-Egypt Invasion the Mother Arc Aqua Blue Ray was not in the Earth core. According to the Guardians, now that our Mother energy is present, we can connect with the Aqualine Sun from the Earth surface, which is the Liquid Luminal plasma light braided into our Earth core and reconnected into the Andromeda Core.

Advanced Souls that have come to this Earth are here to activate what is dormant in other humans and they aren't bent on control or domination, they aren't Ego based or power-hungry. There is nothing wrong with Ego, but our challenge as a species is to align our Ego with our higher self, so that our higher consciousness can be more grounded and available in the physical; without this integration, we stay in duality and we may have the higher thought forms and philosophies, but it isn't going to do much for us unless we fully live it and it becomes a part of our lifestyle.

This is where Alchemy and real transformation happens. The traumas we carry, the exhaustion, DNA damage, the Mother is mending with us. The Venus transits and our movement into the 13th sign has been a part of the repair work and has allowed us access to the quintessence of the Mother, the 5th element that we are now capable of feeling and accessing within.

We are healing thousands of years of manipulation, abuse and infiltration. We are healing Earth grids that have been weaponised and helping to set free trapped Souls, ourselves and future generations. We are finding our divine template and recognizing our true journey is that of Love and re-connecting with our divine Twin Flame, as our Great Mother is experiencing this with the Father and Christ energy she is in union with - fully bringing it into embodiment as Heaven on Earth.

Laura Eisenhower

February 2021

TWIN FLAMES AND THE EVENT WORKBOOK

https://www.jenmccarty.co.uk/books

Jen has written a workbook which is the perfect companion for this sacred text - The Twin Flames and The Event Workbook.

Halfway through writing this book I was very strongly guided by spirit to create a workbook that would accompany this powerful sacred scripture. So therefore I followed this guidance and brought through an amazing offering that will assist you deeply to understand and assimilate all of the information and codes that are shared in this book.

I would highly recommend everybody working with the workbook, as the exercises and meditations work on a deep subconscious level and work with the incredible power of symbols, which are the language of the unconscious mind.

If you really want to experience a shift in your vibrational reality and receive great assistance in truly becoming one with your higher self, then I highly recommend you gift yourself this beautiful workbook that goes alongside this sacred text.

I will now share with you a preview chapter taken from Twin Flames and The Event companion workbook on ***Working with your Inner Child***.

Twin Flames and The Event Workbook

Working with your Inner Child

Inner child work is extremely important for those of us on the spiritual path. Unless you were born to completely enlightened parents, there is not a soul alive who is not suffering to some degree or another from PTSD (Post Traumatic Stress Syndrome), due to being born into this third-dimensional matrix.

We are all, for the most part, brought up by adults who have no recollection of their spiritual heritage, the fact that we are all divine beings, having a temporary human experience.

Because of our care keepers' lack of spiritual knowledge, this has created a huge problem whereby many children have been bought up and have received deeply destructive programming.

As children, we do not have the consciousness to be able to unravel the trauma that happens to us. And so, oftentimes, what happens is that the trauma remains stuck in our energetic field. A perfect analogy to describe this process is a stuck record. If we do not process the trauma that we experience as and when we experience it, then the trauma gets stuck and lodged into our etheric field, and keeps going round and round.

Once this energy is stuck, this means that pranic energy, also known as chi energy is unable to flow freely throughout the vessel. This is one of the by-products of not resolving your childhood trauma.

Another side effect is that very often you attract circumstances that will restimulate the original trauma, which you will experience in your life as a repeated pattern.

At some point on the spiritual path, you will become aware of your own beautiful, sacred inner child and you will remember that our soul consciousness is deeply connected to our eternal child self. And one day, maybe today, you will remember that in the eyes of Mother-Father God, you will always be that sacred divine child.

At some point within our spiritual evolutionary journey, we realize that the child self is the most powerful and most potent aspect of our consciousness and we must do whatever it takes to connect with our inner child and make them feel safe in the world again.

You may think that your inner child is searching for a Twin Flame or a Guru or is wishing that she could go back in time to make her parents perfect parents. But this is simply not true.

What I have discovered is that all that your inner child is searching for is **you**. You are the parental self, and you are the child self and this is connected to the Holy Trinity, the Divine Mother within, the Divine Father within and the Divine Christ/Sophia child.

You are that eternal child and all you have ever been searching for and praying for is your divine adult self.

Twin Flames and The Event Workbook

Exercise upon Working with Your Inner Child

I would like to now share with you some powerful exercises that will enable you to connect very deeply to your child self.

Please take a pen and paper and write out all of the things that you loved to do as a child. Did you love drawing, painting, climbing, doing Lego, playing with dolls, writing or playing at being a teacher? Please take a moment to list all of the things that you loved to do as a child. When you have completed that list, which I would like you to add to often, please make a promise to yourself that you will start doing some of these activities again.

GLOSSARY

3D: 3D refers to the programming or the veil that covers over the earthly plane. We are all divine beings and we are all one with each other. Third-dimensional programming seeks to completely deny this truth and hide the truth of our spiritual heritage and eternal oneness.

4D: Fourth-dimensional consciousness refers to someone who has transcended and awoken out of the spell of the third-dimensional matrix but has not yet reached fifth-dimensional consciousness, which is unity consciousness. Within the fourth dimension, polarity still exists and there are many beings of light and dark. There is a lot of confusion in the fourth dimension but also a lot of power.

5D: In fifth-dimensional consciousness, we are always in sacred Union with our divine counterpart. The fifth dimension is home and is the gateway to full multiple-dimensional consciousnesses. The hallmarks of fifth-dimensional consciousness are ecstasy, unity, bliss, oneness, rapture, heaven, high vibrations, understanding, Gnosis, truth and oneness with all that is.

Alchemical Marriage: Alchemical marriage, also referred to as the Hieros Gamos, also known as the Kundalini merge, is the sacred marriage and merge of the Kundalini energy at the base of the spine. When one incarnates, the Kundalini energy is dormant, which represents duality consciousness at some point within one's awakening. The Kundalini will be triggered to come out of its dormant state into its awakened state and this represents Union consciousness. The alchemical marriage refers to Sacred Union with self and all that is.

Arcturus: Arcturus is a star located in the Bootes constellation. It is considered to be a very old star system. As such, the race of beings from this star system.

Arcturians: The Arcturians are also considered to be old souls. The Arcturians embody wisdom, knowledge and teaching. They enjoy passing on their information and lessons. They are responsible for and are guardians of the Ascension technology.

Ascension: Ascension refers to the transformation of one's consciousness from a 3D caterpillar to a fifth-dimensional butterfly. Ascension refers to the process of one's consciousness transforming from the lead of the ego itself to the gold of the Christed Self. Ascension is when you become one with your higher divine eternal self.

Ashtar Command: The Ashtar Command predicted that those who ascend on the first wave will have the opportunity to return to Earth in an ascended state, to awaken the rest of humanity to the opportunity for Ascension. The Book of Enoch supports this prediction by speaking of the sudden appearance of 144,000 Ascended Masters on Earth, who will transform the world and reject clouds of darkness and despair.

Avatar: An avatar being is your multiple-dimensional higher self, over soul that we are obliged to vibrationally align with, whilst inhabiting these earthly vessels.

Bird Tribe: Bird tribe refers to the 144,000 Starseeds. The Bird Tribe are very often reincarnations of Aboriginal indigenous elders, who are deeply connected to the outer star system such as Pleiades, Arcturus, Andromeda and Sirius to name but a few.

The Book of Gnosis and of Remembrance: The Book of Gnosis and of Remembrance is another way of saying The Akashic records, where all information is stored pertaining to past, present and future timelines. Every breath that is breathed, every sigh that is sighed, every word that is spoken, every thought that is thought, is stored within the Akashic field also known as The Book of Gnosis and of Remembrance.

Book of Revelations: Revelation chapter seven refers to countless numbers of each nation dressed in white robes as John said in the Bible. This could have been his perception of the light bodies that adorn the crowd, following the trail of 144,000 to ascend the second and third waves of Ascension. John also said that these were the ones who were transformed in the time of great upheaval, a seven-year period of a great many trials. This would correspond to the natural disasters that were predicted in order for the Earth to cleanse itself from industrial times before its own ascent.

Catalyst Twin: A Catalyst Twin is the soul that stands next to your tonal counterpart and as such is the closest vibrational match to your true twin flame identical tonal counterpart.

Christ Consciousness: Christ Consciousness refers to The Awakening of one's consciousness to the fact that we are all divine beings, we are all one, we all carry the vibration and codes of the Eternal Christ within us. Christ consciousness is The Awakening that the soul goes through to come home to the remembrance that every single one of God's creations is sacred.

Codons: When I speak about codons, I am referring to light codes that are stored within one's DNA, which are awaiting the moment of a triggering that will activate them to come out of their offline state into their online state.

Faith codes: Faith codes are activated when we stand firmly in our faith and realise that faith is a choice. This is what activates our faith codes. Faith is when we actively choose to have faith, regardless of what we are being presented within the third-dimensional reality.

The Galactic Federation of Light: The Galactic Federation of Light is an alliance of beings from across the galaxy or across galaxies. These creatures are benevolent in nature. The Federation of Light was founded over 4.5 million years ago. It was created to stop inter-dimensional dark forces from taking over the galaxy. Basically, the Galactic Federation of Light is like the Justice League.

The Halls of Amenti: The Halls of Amenti is a time portal passage that holds the race blueprint field that would allow the fragmented Angelic Human souls to eventually re-evolve back into its original divine blueprint as a 12D Krystal being. The Halls of Amenti are six-time portal passages that are dimensional pathways to leave this 3D Earth system. In these "Halls" there are large bound holographic books with all of the hidden human history and where written historical records are kept. You can ask for guidance to the most pertinent information for you at this present time and read the book with your life mission and blueprint inside it. Not all of us will be granted access to the Hall; you must have earned it with sincere inquiry of your soul or past lifetimes of access that have demonstrated your purity to your soul purpose. (This definition is taken from the wonderful Lisa Renée's Ascension glossary.)

Identical Tonal Counterpart: The same definition as a Twin Flame.

Kali Yuga: Earth takes a 360-degree journey through the galaxy every 25,920 years. Each complete cycle is known as Yuga. There are four parts to Yuga. Two parts (180 degrees) of ascending consciousness and two parts (180 degrees) of descending consciousness. The Kali Yuga is the last quadrant of the descending consciousness within the Yuga. The Earth is now on the edge of the Kali Yuga. The biblical name for Kali Yuga is the End of Time. The End of Time will not be the end of the Earth, but the end of darkness and evil on Earth and the dawn of the Seventh Golden Age of Enlightenment.

Karmic partner: Another word for a karmic partner is a bodysuit partner, someone who you have attracted based upon thought forms of lack and limitation. A relationship that will help you see your shadow self and awaken to what you believe you are worthy of. The karmic partner will often show you the very opposite of true love.

The Law of Attraction: The law of attraction is connected to the law of vibration, which is connected to the law of choice. Everything already exists in the universe and it is our responsibility as transmitters to adjust and attune our frequency, to come into alignment with that which we wish to manifest and we do that by experiencing the feeling of the wish already fulfilled.

Magnum Opus: Refers to the great work of the SOUL.

The Matrix: The matrix realm, refers to the third-dimensional programme that has been overlaid upon this earthly realm that has been infused with instructions, pertaining to thoughts and beliefs of lack, limitation and lack of empowerment.

Merkabah: The term Merkabah, spelt M E R K A B A H, means *chariots* in Hebrew. The shape of the Merkabah is two-star tetrahedrons, polarity, duality, male, female, the male tetrahedron and electrical energy. When we access our MERKABAH this means that we have attained a high level of consciousness, and are able to access the Akashic records and memories of our soul's journey throughout many different lifetimes

Monadic Soul Group: All souls are created within a monadic soul structure. Our soul and **Monad** is a family of consciousness that contains all members of our soul group - extensions of our soul consciousness that are existing simultaneously in other dimensional timelines.

The Monkey Mind: The monkey mind refers to be the egoic consciousness that is disconnected from the heart consciousness. The heart consciousness is like a GPS system that knows the fastest, quickest route to one's destiny. The monkey mind is only aware of the moves that are immediately in front of us. The monkey mind is always jumping from one thought to the other and one can never find spiritual stability without a practice that harnesses the monkey mind.

Pleiadians: Pleiadians are humanoids and are considered better-looking versions of us. They nearly always lack pigmentation in their skin and hair, giving them an albino appearance. As a rule, Pleiadians do not carry around much excess fat, although females are known to have curvy figures. They don't usually have curly hair or beards. Indeed humans and Pleiadians share ancestors, since Earth was once a Lyran colony.

The Pleiades Star System: A conspicuous group or cluster of stars in the constellation Taurus; commonly spoken of as seven, though only six are visible.

Samvartaka: The *Mahabharata* tell us Samvartaka Fires emanate from *Surya*, the Sun, and are characterized as a cloud filled with 'wreaths of lightning.' Strange clouds accompany the lightning. It is wonderful to behold… This is the same as the Solar flash event.

Soul mate: A soulmate is someone who is part of your monadic soul group which is comprised of 144 souls - 72 masculine 72 feminine.

A Spiritual Download: A spiritual download can be likened to a computer download. At some point information gets downloaded into our consciousness, which comes from the higher dimensional realms. In other words, a download is information from a higher consciousness, downloaded into our Earth consciousness.

A Starseed: A Starseed is a volunteer soul who has heard the call to return to mother Earth as she is in her Ascension trajectory. A Starseed is a very old ancient soul, who has been specifically chosen for the gifts and the vibrations that they hold, that are specifically related to assisting the collective in this ascension.

Twin Flame: A Twin Flame is your opposite vibrational counterpart that stands opposite you within the monadic soul group structure.

Zero-point field: The Zero-point field is accessed via the present moment. The Zero-point field is the gateway to full multiple-dimensional consciousnesses. When one's consciousness arrives home in the Zero-point field, one remembers one's Avatar consciousness and one's ability and indeed duty to visit alternative dimensional timelines and realities.

The Places Where the 144,000 are Mentioned:

THE 144,000 WARRIORS OF THE LIGHT: The 144,000 Lightworkers were mentioned in the book of Revelation, by the Ashtar Command, Sananda, Native Americans and many others. Many of the 144,000 are coming out of their long spiritual sleep and cellular memories being activated within them; memories reminding us that they reincarnated to be part of this huge planetary shift. Many of the 144,000 are being activated in the Dreamtime and are being visited by the galactic self, empowering them for their upcoming mission in the Great Awakening of planet Earth.

*APPENDIX 1

NOVEMBER 2020 GLOBAL TRANSMISSION*

Twin soul Ascension report: 11:11 gateway

all 144000 twin souls must unite now.

Dearest Brothers and Sisters,

Greetings of the most high. We come forward now in this moment of your time with very important news to share with you - ever-evolving humanity. As many of you are well aware, the energies are now rapidly moving towards the Ascension horizon event of the 21st of the 12th 2020. Please know brothers and sisters there is a great deal of preparatory work that needs to take place within the Ascension community, within the Twin Soul collective, in order to ensure that the highest timeline possible manifests for everybody personally and for the entire collective.

These are truly the most exciting times that any of us could ever be living in and for all of us Starseed Twin Flame way showers, it is so important that we dig deep into our spiritual toolkit at the moment and utilise all of our most potent spiritual tools.

The tools that are the most highly recommended for us all to work with currently are - resting as awareness for short moments - bringing your awareness to the present moment, whenever you naturally remember to do so, committing to a spiritual practice by going on endless rampages of gratitude and counting your blessings tirelessly. Working with the phenomenal tool of Ho'oponopono (I am sorry, I forgive you, thank you, I love you) and also remembering that everybody who has incarnated on the Earth today is experiencing PTSD (Post Traumatic Stress Disorder) to some degree or another.

So it is our absolute duty to go forward in kindness and service to all of our Brothers and Sisters, offering a high vibration and our unconditional presence to whoever we are blessed to be in contact with - whether that be the man at the garage, the lady in the post office or our child's school teacher. It is our duty to hold the higher ground and send forth high and loving vibrations to all of our Brothers and Sisters.

When we make these choices, we quickly align with the vibration of creation, which is ultimately ecstatic and expansive. We are each individual transmitters and if we do not take control of our consciousness, our egoic consciousness has full reign and this is like the blind leading the blind.

Without a spiritual practice there is no possibility of evolving and becoming one with our higher self, but as soon as we commit to a spiritual practice and start orienting our thoughts towards being empty and present and training ourselves to go on rampages of gratitude, then we quickly align with the vibration of creation and we experience miracle after miracle, synchronicity after synchronicity, divine ordained meetings of destiny, abundance and all of the great things that spirit has to offer.

If you are lazy you will not get anywhere on the spiritual path, as enlightenment is an active process. It is not a static plateau that you reach, it is a constant choice - despite the rhetoric of the egoic consciousness, which is perpetually addicted to the victim narrative and to the idea of separation.

We pray deeply that you take on this guidance and commit diligently to your spiritual practice. Your Twin Flame needs you to stabilise in the Zero-point field, fifth dimensional consciousness. Your Twin Flame needs you to come home to your divinity, to come home to your divine self - to remember that you are a Daughter or Son of the most high Mother-Father God, and you and your sacred union represents the highest actualisation of divinity within the universe.

It is so important Brothers and Sisters that you let go of the programmes of doubt that the false dark matrix has imposed upon God's children. You must recognise these programmes and choose not to believe them and buy into them. Indeed you must override them with thoughts of gratitude and service to your Brothers and Sisters.

The message that we would most like to convey in this written transmission is that all of you who are reading these words have an extremely important role in the upcoming ascension of mother Gaia. You have signed up to be the for- runners - the way showers of this ascension that all of God's children are going through. When we use the word Ascension we are referring to the transformation of the third-dimensional caterpillar consciousness to the fifth-dimensional butterfly consciousness - from enslavement to freedom and sovereignty.

We would like to now take a moment to speak to you about the significance of the upcoming 11:11 portal. On the 11:11 transmission we are being guided to facilitate the coming together of every single one of the 144,000 pre-ordained Twin Soul unions that were seeded at the time of Lemuria. We will be working very deeply and diligently to clear any blocks between these pre-ordained sacred unions in order to add an unprecedented amount of momentum to the physicalisation of these extremely important unions, in relation to the Ascension of Mother Gaia.

Every time a genuine Twin Soul union actualises on the physical plane, the codes and the frequencies that are omitted are aligned with the vibrations akin to ecstasy, bliss and rapture. As each Twin Soul pair emits these codes into the collective, please know that it is these frequencies that will literally lift the planet from the third dimension to the fifth dimension.

This is why it is absolutely imperative that the focus is placed again on the importance of the physicalisation of these Twins Soul unions.

Therefore, in the 11:11 transmission, we will be clearing all blocks to enable the swift manifestation of these sacred unions and we will be working with the fifth-dimensional codes of these unions with our galactic Brothers and Sisters from the Pleiades and Arcturus; to literally lift planet Earth from this 3-D lockdown vibration into the fifth-dimensional Golden Age vibration.

We cannot stress enough the importance of those of you who identify as Wayshowers/Starseeds to hold your centre now. Breathe deeply and choose to trust in your divine creator.

You are a divine being of the highest order. You are loved, guarded over and protected, every second of every minute of every moment of your existence.

This is an invitation for you to reach energetically towards that knowing - towards that remembrance of your divinity, that you are so precious, that you are so beloved and you are a child of God.

You have not been abandoned and all of your deepest prayers are being worked on right now by our creator and if you feel emotional reading these words, this is confirmation from your high self that this is absolute truth.

Social media is transforming right before our very eyes. Nefarious energies have taken over many of the social media platforms and therefore it is so important that we all gravitate towards more cleaner, higher vibrational social media platforms.

I have now moved to Mighty Network and I will be sharing all of my content from there from now on.

It is an incredibly high vibrational, clean platform that was created due to all of the censorship that was taking place on all the popular social media platforms. It is a safe place for all of us Starseed Lightworkers and I very much look forward to welcoming you all into my Mighty Network community.

Have faith Brothers and Sisters, see with your heart, remember with your heart, **we are so loved and the light has already won.**

In love and eternal light

Jenji and the White Wolf Tribe.

BOOK REVIEW PAGE

PLEASE LEAVE A REVIEW ON AMAZON IF YOU HAVE ENJOYED THIS BOOK

It is my deepest and sincere prayer that this book has given you a profound understanding of Twin Flames and The Event. I hope you will find this book to be a valuable go-to source for any questions you may have regarding your Divine Union.

If you have enjoyed this book and found it helpful, please consider leaving a review on Amazon. Your reviews are hugely helpful to me as an Independent Author and will help others be able to find this book in the Amazon search results.

Thank you, brothers and sisters, for all your support.

LITTLE BOOK OF ATTRACTION

https://www.jenmccarty.co.uk/books

I would like to share with you all now an excerpt from one of the most powerful books I've ever read, which happens to be a book that I created in 2011. It is my go-to book if I ever have a wobble which is very rare since 2013 but it is filled with so many codes that will immediately bring you back to stability in higher consciousness. The book consists of an introduction whereby I share with you all my downloads about how to work very deeply and powerfully with the law of attraction and the rest of the book is a combination of quotes and affirmations from well-known people that have worked successfully with the law of attraction.

Please see below for an excerpt:

"This is a book of miracles, a tale of timeless truth and a promise to the most ancient part of ourselves to remember and align with the highest vibration of who we are.

This is your eternal self knocking at your door. There are gifts and promises encoded in these pages that will, if you allow them to, unlock the timeless wisdom you carry within you.

We are all master creators and we create everything we see and experience in our physical reality from the predominant thoughts *and feelings* we send out. We are vibrational beings, much like a radio transmitter; whatever we experience as our reality, is a direct reflection of the frequencies we emit.

We all possess innate powers to manifest the health, wealth, relationships and careers we desire and the fastest way to actualise this, is through a dedicated and regular practice of Gratitude."

Here is a sample of some of the quotes that are featured in the book:

"If you wish to find the secrets of the universe think of energy, frequency and vibration."

~ Nikola Tesla

"Einstein proved that everything in the universe is energy. All energy vibrates at particular frequencies. We are energy too and so each of us is also vibrating at a frequency. Your thoughts, feelings and beliefs determine the vibration and frequency of your energy."

~ Rhonda Byrne

"There is no matter as such. All matter originates and exists only by virtue of a force which brings the particles of an atom to a vibration and holds this most minute solar system of the atom together. We must assume that behind this force is the existence of a conscious and intelligent mind. This mind is the matrix of all matter."

~ Max Planck

HERE IS THE LINK TO

PURCHASE THE BOOK

https://www.jenmccarty.co.uk/books

*SPIRITUAL RESOURCES AND TRAININGS FROM JEN *

Jen is very excited to be branching out with her spiritual work in order to share the original and powerful healing modalities that her higher self has shared with her.

MONTHLY GLOBAL TRANSMISSIONS

https://www.jenmccarty.co.uk/product/global-transmissions/

Since 2016 Jen has been hosting regular global transmissions on numerological portal dates such as 2:2, 3:3, 4:4 etc. Also on Pagan holidays such as Samhain Imbolc, Equinox and Solstice. The reason for this is that it is so important that the Awakened Star Crew gather together on powerful dates such as these in order to align our will and intention with the will and intention of Mother-Father God.

The ceremonies are a huge part of Jen's mission and she would love all of you reading these words to come and join our amazing Ground Crew Community who show up to take part in these ceremonies regularly.

You will find all the details to join these global ceremonies on the website;

https://www.jenmccarty.co.uk

Many people report an immediate up-levelling in their spiritual vibration, through taking part in the Global

Transmissions and this is due to the potency of gathering with hundreds of people and aligning our intentions with the intentions of our creator.

Most people experience massive shifts, particularly with regards to what is keeping them stuck at a lower vibrational level.

After and sometimes during these Transmissions people can get very emotional and can start crying due to clearing the energies and emotions that no longer serve them. This is a process of bringing the emotions to the surface and then releasing them, and it is always very important to trust that the process is happening in accordance with your Higher Self.

Most people find themselves listening to the Transmissions more than once because each time they listen to it, they find it continues to raise their vibration even higher and assist with shifting more toxic emotions. Please visit:

https://www.jenmccarty.co.uk

Every day, Jen receives hundreds of messages and emails from people from all over the world, thanking her for her profound service to humanity.

Here is an example of the feedback Jen receives on a regular basis after hosting one of her large global ceremonies:

"Hi Jen, I loved last night's ceremony. Just wanted to say all your ceremonies have literally raised my kundalini. I have flashes, cracks, rushes and full-blown activations

every time... just wanted to say as it is so special to me and it is an affirmation for you that you are working your powerful magic... Blessings, protection and loads of love to you xxx"

"I have just done the ceremony on replay.....WOW!!! It was amazing, lots of kundalini shaking and shivering.....thank you Jen - KS"

"The transmission was so powerful and beautiful! Thank you so much Jen! I am still new to follow you and your work, so this was only my second opportunity to participate in one of your transmissions. I really felt the cleansing, healing and support of Archangel Michael and Saint Germain."

"For years I've had pain between my shoulder blades and last night I finally felt it released and surrendered. I felt such pure, unconditional love and once we came to unite in the light with our Divine counterparts, my face was filled with a huge smile and tears were just rolling and flowing out of me to cleanse and purify. I felt pure light and love emanating throughout my whole being. - JV"

"Jen, it was one of the greatest experiences I've ever had in meditation—truly powerful portals of 5D opened up and shifted this realm profoundly. So grateful! And I feel so blessed to participate with you live. Just spectacular! Sending you angel kisses - KK"

Here is the link to book onto the next global transmission:

https://www.jenmccarty.co.uk/product/global-transmissions/

EXCLUSIVE MEMBERSHIP COMMUNITY

THE EVENT IS HAPPENING

Jen will soon be launching an exclusive online membership programme on the Mighty Networks platform for those who have purchased her book and she will continue to update her book material in this group, which will have various levels of membership available: Gold, Silver and Bronze.

So far the feedback from everyone that has read the book prior to its publication has been absolutely unprecedented. So many people are reporting experiencing a huge shift in consciousness. Long-term health issues are being cleared, lucid dreams, out-of-body experiences, and many are being miraculously contacted by their Twin flame out of the blue.

This is due to the fact that the frequencies within this sacred text are transformative in nature and will create an alchemical shift in your spiritual vibration.

Because of the power and potency of this book I've been guided by spirit to create a membership platform that will work as a support group for all the people that have read the book.

This will be a central hub where you can come and share your experiences, be they out-of-body experiences, be they lucid dreams, be they the fact that you have been randomly contacted by your Twin flame after five years of silence.

There will be three different levels and each level will have different offerings.

To receive subsequent updates to this book and Twin Flames and The Event, therefore, please consider becoming a member of The Event is Happening on Mighty Networks, and joining Jen's membership program.

https://www.jenmccarty.co.uk/memberships

Membership benefits vary depending on which tier you sign up for. Here are some examples of the membership benefits

Membership Benefits

- Access a library of recordings of previous Global Transmissions
- Exclusive savings and early access to events/ trainings/Global Transmissions before the general public
- Monthly tarot readings
- Meditations on a number of topics, i.e. Connect with Your Inner Child, Faith Codes, etc.
- Jen will read exclusive excerpts from her up-and-coming books

- "Ask Jen Anything" live webinars
- Private group discussions immediately following each live Global Transmission
- Deep explorations into the mysteries of the Twin Soul phenomenon
- Concentrated and focused support from your peers
- MP3 recordings of Sacred Activations
- Exclusive memes
- Many powerful and pertinent soul gifts

Visit The Event is Happening Membership Group:

https://jen-mccarty.mn.co/feed

Visit The Event is Happening Membership Plan Information Page:

https://www.jenmccarty.co.uk/memberships

TWIN FLAME SACRED ACTIVATION SERIES

https://www.jenmccarty.co.uk/product-category/mp3-activation-series/

In addition to the Transmissions, Jen has been guided by Spirit to produce specific transmissions which address certain topics affecting the collective consciousness. This makes it much easier for people to be able to choose which area of their life they wish to work on, to address their personal challenges. For example: reclaiming your self-worth and healing sexual trauma.

These activations attune you specifically to fifth-dimensional consciousness – the feedback and results so far have been truly mind-blowing, with many people reporting crying the deepest tears they have ever known and many people have said they were then being miraculously contacted by their Twin Flame around the time of completing these activations.

Here is a list of activations which are available to download in MP3 format at time of press:

- Meet the Fifth Dimension Aspect of Your Twin Flame
- Zero Point Activation
- Self-Worth Activation
- Abundance Activation

- Yeshua and Magdalene Divine Union Template
- Atlantis Meditation
- Waterfall
- Inner Child
- Body Transmission
- Light Language Dispensation
- Deep Relaxation
- Rebalance Giving with Receiving
- Source Frequency Activation
- Reviving the Frozen Garden of your Heart
- Angelic T Cell
- Catalyst Twin Clearing

I also have two special activations, one is called the "Yoni Nidra" and the other is called "Miracle Healing for Chronic Illness." These are long in-depth healing meditations that will massively affect your healing journey and spiritual vibration.

The Yoni Nidra MP3 is a powerful visualisation exercise that will enable you to connect deeply with your Yoni (vagina) if you are a divine feminine.

There are very powerful and potent codes within this visualisation which will assist you to shift huge amounts of trauma and abuse personally and collectively that you may have stored within your womb area.

Many people report having miraculous healings with their sexuality, for example, having a much heightened orgasmic potential. It has also helped many beloved's come into union with their next to soul partner.

I really highly recommend working with the Yoni Nidra MP3.

https://www.jenmccarty.co.uk/product-category/mp3-activation-series/

BECOME A CERTIFIED

QUANTUM TIME TRAVEL TECHNIQUE PRACTITIONER

Quantum Time Travel Technique Training

Practitioner Levels I & II

https://www.jenmccarty.co.uk/product/qttt-practitioner-training-program/

The Quantum Time Travel Technique (QTTT) is a technique that Jen has brought through that she uses in many of her 1-to-1 sessions.

This is a paradigm-shifting tool that can effortlessly slip into your healing practice to ensure once and for all that all major deep core issues are cleared entirely from you and your client's field forever!

Jen's intention with this powerful Ascension training is to provide people with the ability to offer 1-to-1 healing sessions with their clients.

QTTT will work alongside many healing modalities such as Reiki, Acupuncture, Theta Healing, Womb Work, Sexuality Healing and any other spiritual alignment work.

Jen is very keen to bring QTTT to the world, as it will bring so much healing which is greatly needed at the moment. Earth is going through so many shifts currently and so many people are healing from deep, unprocessed processed trauma, particularly from their childhood.

QTTT is an accelerated healing modality that has been brought forth in order to deeply support the collective in clearing huge quantities of traumatised and stuck energy.

The Quantum Time Travel Technique teaches:

- The basic principles of counselling a client in a session
- How to hold space for a client - what this means and what this entails
- Take your client on a healing journey – taking their future self to meet their past traumatised and frozen self
- How to identify and release core trauma
- Completely set the child-self free
- Enable emotional healing to take place, so that the client's growth trajectory may begin
- Graduation ceremony

Join live trainings facilitated by Jen via online webinars. In these training sessions there are plenty of opportunities to practice on fellow students, ensuring that they come away feeling positive and confident with regards to facilitating their own healing sessions.

All Certified QTTT Practitioners have not only found they have benefited from the amazing healing benefits of this technique but also experienced the most amazing feedback on the healing benefits received by their clients.

Below is some of the latest feedback which Jen received following the graduation ceremony recently held for her first training of QTTT Level 1 in November 2020:

"I have been through a lot of serious trauma in my life and worked on this for many years in different ways. I have also trained to guide others and help them deal with their own issues. Up until QTTT I had never experienced a way of doing things that really integrated the past traumatised self, that part that was blocked and stuck and how to bring the whole me back together! The times for endless psychotherapy and endlessly going round in circles is long, long gone. Those ways don't help most people, they just keep the old pain going. I felt called to start my practise again, as I know that when the truth of these times comes out (disclosure) there will be a lot of people needing help. Something was holding me back, Spirit said wait, so I waited and then came QTTT!"

The QTTT training ran for the first time in October 2020 and will run again in 2021 and will be facilitated via live webinar sessions over a six-week period. Jen already has a waiting list of people who have benefited from this amazing healing modality and are eager to learn the technique for themselves, either to serve as an additional therapy to integrate into their current healing work or for those who wish to learn the technique, so that they may use it on their friends and family.

Since QTTT Level 1 Practitioner Training was such an amazing success, Jen decided to develop Level II which explores QTTT at a much deeper level. In QTTT II we will be accessing a much deeper exploration into alternative modalities that can be used with this technique, such as working with one's future self - working with the spirit of ancestors that have passed and working with the spirit of one's Twin Flame, including working with totems ascended to masters and archangels. Most if not all candidates who have completed Level I have already signed up for the pre-book list for Level II.

All certified practitioners will be listed on Jen's website **https://www.jenmccarty.co.uk** which receives a high volume of traffic each month and therefore is a great space to promote your services as a Qualified QTTT Practitioner.

To learn more about the Quantum Time Travel Technique,to find a practitioner in your area, or to find out more about training to become a QTTT Certified Practitioner visit:

https://www.jenmccarty.co.uk/product/qttt-practitioner-training-program/

Please visit the website and look at the video testimonials, as it has a lot of information about the benefits QTTT can bring to your life.

MEET YOUR BELOVED

SPIRITUAL MASTERY

ONLINE TRAINING COURSE

https://www.jenmccarty.co.uk/product/4-week-spiritual-mastery-course/

This is one of the most powerful offerings that Jen has brought through and every person that has done the course has gone on to fully stabilize in fifth dimensional consciousness, and has become a teacher, leader, and wayshower - building their own Communities and becoming a role model within them.

This is an extremely powerful course whereby Jen literally holds your hand and walks you into 5th Dimensional consciousness. Sharing with you, all of the tools and techniques and practices that she used to be fully stabilised in 5th dimensional consciousness since October 2013.

This course has been created to assist you on an exceptionally deep level, to align vibrationally with the frequencies of fifth dimensional consciousness. This is an extremely powerful offering that has been brought through in divine timing, to assist those of you who identify as Twin Flame Starseeds. You will be given powerful tools which will assist you to rise up as the illuminated beacon that you have come here to be.

The course comes in four parts. Each part will include a darshan (which is a sacred discourse on the week's subject matter), a powerful visualisation (to assist you to crucially clear many old false beliefs) and the course most importantly includes homework for you to carry out each week, which will train you to formulate new patterns and habits that are in alignment with fifth dimensional consciousness.

The whole purpose of the course is to educate you and remind you, that in order to fully stabilise in higher dimensional consciousness, it is absolutely imperative that you are empowered to take actions every single day that are in alignment with fifth dimensional consciousness.

I invite you to open your heart and open your palms to receive this guidance, as for many of you, this is what your higher selves are very much wanting to deliver to you at this particular conjecture on your evolutionary cycle. And for many of you, you will find that following through with the teachings of this course, will be the answer to your deepest prayers.

It is time now for those who promised to be the illuminated ones, the enlightened ones and the way-showers to step forward now, embodying their full spiritual mastery.

Here is the link to purchase the 4-week spiritual mastery course

https://www.jenmccarty.co.uk/product/4-week-spiritual-mastery-course/

Spiritual Mastery Testimonial

"This is my testimony of how POWERFUL jen mccarty's 4 week spiritual mastery course is! Since receiving just before Xmas, I have to say the "jewels' ' of self mastery information are amazing and if you know anything about this Twin Flame journey, you will know that full self mastery and self love is what brings you into union.

I'm on my 2nd time listening to it and putting the homework into practise. I have to say my connection to Self and Source is so much stronger. I am always seeing 33, 44, 55, 222, 333, 444, 555 and 144. I am grounding myself into the present moment a lot more, BELIEVING in the power of my imagination and so much more.

"I don't want to give too much away. I just want to say to anyone who is genuinely needing help on their spiritual path, this 4 week course is the key and is worth every penny."

I have to be honest I always wanted to buy the course but my financial situation would not have allowed me to for now. Obviously Source knew I needed this and it would propel me into alignment and I actually won the course, little old me who never wins anything. Talk about Divine intervention and timing lol.

But again, I can't stress enough how amazing this course is, Thank you Jen McCarty, you are doing such amazing work, may God continue to bless you."

TESLA TECHNOLOGY - HEALY MACHINE

https://www.jenmccarty.co.uk/healy-machine

The Healy is a bio-resonance tool that works to support your body's energetic field and promote deep cellular healing.

The Healy is a small, very complex piece of equipment. Using precise frequencies and low intensity currents, the Healy works to reverse the process of decreasing cell voltage by restoring the natural voltage of the cell membrane.

Compromised cells lead us to experience a debilitating range of different symptoms, such as the inability to concentrate, learning difficulties, stress/burnout, physical diseases and illness, slow recovery from injury, cellulite, skin breakouts, mental health challenges and emotional instability.

Recently I was very privileged to be invited to be part of the team that has brought through the Healy device. This is incredible Tesla Technology that works with the principle of vibrational frequencies.

A few days ago my friend reached out to me and asked me if I had heard of the Healy machine and she told me that she was diagnosed as being in full-blown menopause. She had had blood tests and a full doctor's analysis which confirmed that she is in full-blown menopause.

She had one session whereby the practitioner sent her some specific resonances for hormones and after having no period for a long time, her period came back in fewer than five days.

I was really blown away when I heard this and it touched something deep inside of me to go and explore what is the Healy.

I was then led to the Healy testimony page and I have no words that can adequately express how blown away I am by the testimonies...

As you may know I have not got behind any products since I launched my offerings to the world and that is because I've never found a product that I 100% resonate with, but I know that I found this with the Healy.

Based on the testimonies that I read I decided to go ahead and buy the Healy.

There seems to be a huge buzz in the UK with lots and lots of people being ready to purchase and jump on board the Healy train...

It is such a phenomenal investment on all levels spiritually, physically and financially I made my money back within 24 hours of purchasing the machine and they even sent me a brand-new Healy machine which I have given to my assistant.

Here is a link to all products:

https://www.healyworld.net/en/the-product-world/

Healy Testimonies

I will now include some testimonies from the feedback page and the link to the feedback page...

https://www.facebook.com/groups/645513899543603

I honestly thought Healy was something I'd try and send back as I was very skeptical. I'm only on day 12 of using it and I'm off my daily antihistamines for hay fever and miraculously I am sleeping all night without two sleeping pills that I have been on for over 10 years!!! If I ever went without them I would lie wide awake all night having hot and cold sweats. I am gobsmacked! I don't understand HOW it works but it DOES work.

Still waiting for my Healy but my girlfriend is doing distant healing which I have benefited from immensely. An incredible pain left in an incredible three minutes flat.

So the other day I was in so much pain and my friend ran the pain program for me. He is in NC and I am in AZ. I could feel warmth flooding the area. It was so healing, I fell asleep and the pain was gone, increasing my energy and confidence and decreasing pain after years of chronic fatigue.

In answer to the question what do you love most about your Healy? That it can help so many people and animals, with health, vitality and overall wellbeing!

Or I place them on positive words while vibrating matching frequencies. For this I'm mainly placing them on the words: "Self love and acceptance" as a Time-Waver practitioner has made me a program for this.

Final words: I've been very impressed with the level of support that I have received in terms of learning how to use the device and also how to operate the back office when it comes to signing up new members.

For all of you who are ready to jump on board now and make the most of this offer that is going to end as soon as possible here is the link for you to buy the Healy machine...

Please email me at cosmicgypsy33@gmail.com to receive more information on the Healy machine - alternatively please click this link

https://www.healyworld.net/en/the-product-world/

If you are wanting to purchase a Healy machine please use the link below with my name. This means that you will be added onto my team and will benefit from my large community.

https://partner.healyworld.net/jenmccarty144

https://www.jenmccarty.co.uk/healy-machine

Please turn to the back page for all the QR Codes for Jen's offerings

USEFUL CONTACT INFORMATION

BOOK IMAGE ARTIST: Cheryl Yambrach Rose

Cheryl is a portrait painter, visionary artist, and the author of the book "Art Through the Eyes of the Soul" (foreword by Dr. Jean Houston). She paints in oils on linen in a synthesis of the Old Master style and her own unique technique of tuning in through the eyes. Excelling in spiritual portraiture, Cheryl is collected by many discerning luminaries, including Gary Zukav and Neale Donald Walsch. Her artwork has been published and shown worldwide, including in the Nelson Rockefeller Collection, the Rosicrucian Egyptian Museum, and the San Francisco Palace of Fine Arts. It has been featured on the Wisdom and Travel Channels, and is included in a book of the top 100 living Western Artists. In England, she has been published by Thames and Hudson, Blandford, Watkin's, and others. She is featured in the Chinese film "Awakening Journey" which also features Neale Donald Walsch and Dr. Bruce Lipton. Her oracle deck "Art Through the Eyes of the Soul" (Blue Angel Publishing) has been translated into French, Chinese, Japanese, Czech, and German. The oracle deck "Art Through the Starstream" won a 'Visionary Product of the Year' award at INATS in Denver in 2016. A new oracle deck, "Transcendent Journeys," was published by Blue Angel in 2020.

Her spiritual portraits are multi-dimensional paintings incorporating information accessed through the sight of the pineal gland or inner eye as it connects to the Source Field. Her Neo-Mythic Art® brings forth images out of the morphic fields surrounding sacred sites and the vortices within them. She lives and works in Glastonbury, England, Prague, Czech Republic, and Mt. Shasta, California. In Prague she is co-founder with her husband of Daghda Vision s.r.o., a company dedicated to global cultural exchange, art, film and publishing.

"As an artist my highest aspiration is the infusion of Spirit into matter."

WEBSITE: www.cherylrose.com

SOCIAL MEDIA:

https://www.facebook.com/cherylrosehall/

BOOK AFTERWORD: Laura Eisenhnower

Laura Eisenhower is a Global Alchemist, Researcher and Medical and Intuitive Astrologist. She is an internationally acclaimed speaker who has presented her work worldwide. Laura is the great-granddaughter of President Dwight David Eisenhower and she reveals Exopolitical information about his administration that has been largely held in secrecy. She is considered by many to be one of North America's leading researchers on Health, Exopolitics, Alchemy, Metaphysics, and Galactic History.

Laura works to free us from the 3-D holographic time-loop, False Archonic systems and Military Industrial Complex and exposes hidden agendas so we can take our power back. Feeling a calling regarding her mission since she was a child, she has gained incredible insight through her wilderness adventures, psychic development and has been connecting major dots about how to guide us into higher Earth energies.

She has a deep understanding of Gaia-Sophia and our Divine Blueprint and how they connect to the Venus transits, Earth grids, Global Alchemy, DNA and ET races. Her passion is to inspire unity consciousness and bring us back to the Zero-point/Unified field, the totality of our divine powers.

WEBSITE: https://cosmicgaia.org/

SOCIAL MEDIA:
https://www.facebook.com/laura.magdaleneeisenhower

JEN MCCARTY

Widely known as the Healer of the Healers - Jen McCarty has earned the most astonishing place in everyone's heart. Jen assists people with addiction recovery, as well as helping many people heal their core wounds on a soul level. Jen had a massive life-changing Kundalini Awakening when she was just 21, in the Himalayas in Northern India, chanting the mantra "Om Namah Shivaya." From that moment on she passed over the threshold from third-dimensional consciousness to stabilising in fifth-dimensional consciousness.

Jen has since devoted her whole adult life serving her Brothers and Sisters and has been blessed with a massive amount of extremely dedicated followers over the last five years and has built up a social media following of over 175,000 people.

Jen specialises in working with the reunion of Twin Flames and the removal of roadblocks that stand in the way of that. She is an awakened spiritual teacher, deeply and highly skilled at facilitating a space for all those who she comes into contact with. She has a phenomenal track record in uniting many, many Twin Flames, assisting them to connect with their multi-dimensional aspect and activating the Hieros Gamos – the inner alchemical marriage of the masculine and feminine energies within, and very skilfully identifying and removing all blocks that stand in the way of triumphant Twin Flame Union.

Jen has been working quite specifically with the Twin Flame Community and her skills are vast and varied – she can help bring in greater levels of abundance, greater health, wellbeing, weight loss and also assists people to align with their soul's highest density.

Jen has earned access to the Akashic Records through the purification of her own heart, through her own personal Ascension process. This enables her to bring forth potent wisdom in order to assist you in successfully completing the lessons you incarnated to master.

Jen has facilitated a number of global spiritual retreats which were hosted recently at Glastonbury and Mount Shasta.

Many consider working with Jen McCarty truly the fast track to spiritual awakening and Twin Flame reunion. The results of Jen's work so far has been truly mind-blowing. Her monthly Global Transmissions are regularly attended by 800+ fellow spiritual seekers and many people say that she has become one of the world's leading change makers in the spiritual community, assisting her beloved Brothers and Sisters to discover the harmony and alignment with God Consciousness that they have been perpetually seeking.

Many of Jen's community feel absolutely blessed and fortunate to have the opportunity to connect with Jen in a personal setting. Since Jen's community has gone from strength to strength, she is unable to spend time counselling individual clients due to the waiting lists becoming too long.

Jen wants to be able to assist as many people as possible and therefore her membership community was born to serve the collective, as opposed to using up all her energy on individual sessions.

JOIN JEN'S SACRED COMMUNITIES ON SOCIAL MEDIA

THE EVENT IS HAPPENING TELEGRAM GROUP

https://t.me/Theeventishappening

YOUTUBE JEN MCCARTY COSMIC GYPSY

https://www.youtube.com/channel/UC_8fJz5gA nhRqZ740QXlzmw

GAB JEN JEN 144

https://gab.com/jenjen144

MEWE JEN MCCARTY

https://mewe.com/i/jenmccarty2

TWITTER JEN MCCARTY144

https://twitter.com/jen_mccarty

INSTAGRAM TWIN FLAMES AND THE EVENT

https://www.instagram.com/twinflamesandtheevent/

FACEBOOK THE EVENT IS HAPPENING GROUP

https://www.facebook.com/groups/theeventishappening

FACEBOOK JEN MCCARTY

https://www.facebook.com/jen.mccarty.75/

QR CODES

Please download any free QR Code scanning app on your smart phone and scan the codes below for quick access to Jen's offerings.

4 WEEK SPIRITUAL MASTERY

https://www.jenmccarty.co.uk/product/4-week-spiritual-mastery-course/

QTTT TRAINING

https://www.jenmccarty.co.uk/product/qttt-practitioner-training-program/

MP3 ACTIVATION SERIES

https://www.jenmccarty.co.uk/product-category/mp3-activation-series/

THE EVENT IS HAPPENING MEMBERSHIP GROUP

https://www.jenmccarty.co.uk/memberships

AUTHOR / BOOKS PAGE

https://www.jenmccarty.co.uk/books

HEALY MACHINE

https://www.jenmccarty.co.uk/healy-machine

GLOBAL TRANSMISSIONS

https://www.jenmccarty.co.uk/product/global-transmissions/

Made in the USA
Monee, IL
16 April 2021

65936395R00166